# Vietnamese Americans

## Westview Replica Editions

This book is a Westview Replica Edition. The concept of Replica Editions is a response to the crisis in academic and informational publishing. Library budgets for books have been severely curtailed; economic pressures on the university presses and the few private publishing companies primarily interested in scholarly manuscripts have severely limited the capacity of the industry to properly serve the academic and research communities. Many manuscripts dealing with important subjects, often representing the highest level of scholarship, are today not economically viable publishing projects. Or, if they are accepted for publication, they are often subject to lead times ranging from one to three years. Scholars are understandably frustrated when they realize that their first-class research cannot be published within a reasonable time frame, if at all.

Westview Replica Editions are our practical solution to the problem. The concept is simple. We accept a manuscript in camera-ready form and move it immediately into the production process. The responsibility for textual and copy editing lies with the author or sponsoring organization. If necessary we will advise the author on proper preparation of footnotes and bibliography. We prefer that the manuscript be typed according to our specifications, though it may be acceptable as typed for a dissertation or prepared in some other clearly organized and readable way. The end result is a book produced by lithography and bound in hard covers. Initial edition sizes range from 400 to 600 copies, and a number of recent Replicas are already in second printings. We include among Westview Replica Editions only works of outstanding scholarly quality or of great informational value, and we will continue to exercise our usual editorial standards and quality control.

# Vietnamese Americans: Patterns of Resettlement and Socioeconomic Adaptation in the United States

## Darrel Montero

As of November 1978, more than 170,000 Indochinese refugees had come to the United States after a traumatic flight from their native land, arriving with little preparation for the changes they would face. This book documents and analyzes this unique migration and, employing data from a national sample, reports on the changing socioeconomic status of the Vietnamese refugees. Dr. Montero presents and analyzes data on the refugees' employment, education, income, receipt of federal assistance, and proficiency in the English language; his model of Spontaneous International Migration (SIM) places the Vietnamese immigration experience in a broader sociohistorical context. He has found that, despite the myriad of problems the newcomers have faced, they have been adapting successfully to life in the United States, and in only three years have made remarkable social and economic progress.

Darrel Montero, associate professor and director of the Urban Ethnic Research Program, Arizona State University, was previously assistant professor of urban studies and director of the Urban Ethnic Research Program at the University of Maryland, College Park.

Chân-thành cảm-ta tất cả những ngườì Viêt-Nam
dã bỏ thì giờ quý báu dể giúp
tôi hoàn-tất quyển sách này.


I am indebted to all the Vietnamese who
so generously gave of their time
to make this volume possible.

# Vietnamese Americans: Patterns of Resettlement and Socioeconomic Adaptation in the United States

Darrel Montero

Foreword by Chau Kim Nhan

Westview Press / Boulder, Colorado

*A Westview Replica Edition*

Copyright © 1979 by Westview Press, Inc.

Published in 1979 in the United States of America by
  Westview Press, Inc.
  5500 Central Avenue
  Boulder, Colorado 80301
  Frederick A. Praeger, Publisher

Library of Congress Catalog Card Number: 78-21771
ISBN: 0-89158-264-9

Printed and bound in the United States of America

For Tara and David—
and Judy

# Table of Contents

# Preface

For years the story of Asians in America has held great fascination for me. Since 1971, when I joined the Japanese American Research Project at the University of California, Los Angeles (UCLA), I have studied Asian Americans with increasing respect and admiration. The remarkable socioeconomic progress of Japanese Americans in the face of adversity is a stunning success story. My involvement in that research project has led me quite naturally to an interest in other Asian immigrant groups and most recently to the resettlement of some 170,000 Vietnamese refugees in the United States.

I soon learned that little research had been conducted on these new arrivals. After much digging at the Interagency Task Force for Indochina Refugees and after much correspondence with the handful of scholars conducting research on the Vietnamese, I have pieced together what I believe is a large and rich source of data. These data will, I think, be invaluable to scholars conducting research on Vietnamese resettlement in the United States. It is with this objective in mind that I have written this volume, provided supplementary tables, and prepared a selected bibliography on the Vietnamese experience in America.

This book is the result of the efforts of a great many people. It is with pleasure that I acknowledge their valuable contributions:

Gene N. Levine, Kenneth D. Bailey, Ralph H. Turner, and the late Leo Reeder, my mentors at UCLA.

Lynne Rienner, Executive Editor at Westview Press, and Miriam Gilbert, also of Westview Press, whose encouragement and expertise kept this project on track.

Professors Hisachi Hirayama and Dong Soo Kim, co-directors of the Vietnamese Resettlement Project at the University of Tennessee, Memphis; William Tuchrello of the Library of Congress (Southeast Asian collection); Professor William T. Liu; Dr. Elena Yu; Edward Sponga of the HEW Refugee Task Force; Roy S. Bryce-Laporte, Director, and Stephen R. Couch, Research Coordinator of the Research Institute on Immigration and Ethnic Studies, Smithsonian Institution; Nguyen Duy Hy; Nguyen Minh Chau, Project Director for Opportunity Systems, Inc., for providing valuable reference materials.

Chau Kim Nhan, Ellen McLaughlin, Larry McLaughlin, and Professor Bette Woody, for their careful reading of the entire manuscript, and for their many excellent suggestions and comments.

Carol Boyer, Susan Nelson, Jane Stokes, and Kay Huke, for their careful editing.

Beth Elliott, Sandra Hollan, and Annette Vecchiarelli for their skillful typing of numerous drafts of the volume.

The University of Maryland's Institute for Urban Studies, for its good-natured support throughout the writing of this volume. And Tom Davenport, my research assistant, who made many trips to the University library.

I would like to gratefully acknowledge the contributions of my friend and colleague Judith McDowell. Judy has played a major role in both the development and conceptualization of the volume. She has painstakingly reviewed each and every draft of the manuscript as it developed. Without her skills the volume would not have been completed in a timely manner.

Finally, I wish to thank my parents, whose respect for learning and whose self-sacrifice was my first inspiration, and my wife, Tara McLaughlin, who never failed to provide her technical and professional skills at a moment's notice, and whose encouragement made it all possible.

January 1979                    Darrel Montero

                                College Park

# Foreword

BY CHAU KIM NHAN

In 1954, the Geneva Agreements split Vietnam into two parts and allowed the Vietnamese to decide within six months whether to choose as their residence either the North or the South. At the deadline, about one million Vietnamese from the North chose to be resettled in the South.

The reasons most of these refugees gave for leaving were that they had witnessed the mistreatment of their relatives or friends at the hands of the Communists. During the years they lived under the Communist regime, the Vietnamese in the North were constantly in fear of persecution and arrest, without trial.

In 1975, another mass evacuation occurred, before the take-over of Saigon by the Communists. Asked why they left the country now that the war was over and Vietnam had recovered independence and unity, the first refugees who arrived in the United States in May 1975 explained:

> We love our country. We don't want to be far from home, from our ancestors' tombs, our relatives, our friends. And we knew before leaving Vietnam that life would not be easy abroad. But we had no choice, because conditions of living

xiii

under the new regime are unbearable. You will see, more people will get out of the country.

And they added that they had experienced the Communist regime before. They had witnessed the Communist atrocities during the war against the French, the summary executions, persecutions for religious beliefs, inhumane conditions in their prisoner camps, and the mass killings during the Tet offensive of 1968. These refugees were afraid of what would happen when the Communists took over the South and panic ensued when the armed forces retreated from the Highlands in March 1975.

The real mass evacuation began with the airlift in April 1975. Everyday, I witnessed several transport aircrafts leaving from the International Tan Son Nhat Airport in Saigon carrying U.S. Embassy employees and their dependents to Guam and the Philippines. On Monday, April 28, 1975, when the runway was damaged by Communist shelling, a fleet of helicopters flew in to pick up the people who were waiting inside the U.S. Embassy compound. However, when the last helicopter took off from the roof of the U.S. Embassy, hundreds of people were left behind.

After three years of living under the new regime, more and more people have escaped from Vietnam, defying the Coast Guard and braving the storms of the monsoon season. Before they fled, they understood the dangers they would face at sea and they accepted the risks willingly and courageously. Thousands of people died from hunger and thirst on the ocean, and hundreds of boats sank, along with their human cargo. Those who did not die en route made their way to Thailand, Malaysia, Indonesia, and the Philippines, where more than 100,000 refugees are still in camps.

The Vietnamese, like the Cambodians and Laotians, have been allowed into the United States under Section 212(d)(5) (66 Stat. 188; 8USC #1182 (d) (5)) of the Immigration and Nationality Act of 1952 and subsequent revisions. While they are legally similar to other aliens waiting for immigrant visas under special programs, they have been treated differently from other immigrants in one respect: the U.S. government has resettled the Vietnamese into American society during the waiting period. Fortunately, on October 28, 1977, the Congress passed Public Law 95-145 authorizing the refugees to become permanent residents upon request. This new status will enable them to apply for citizenship status in five years, to begin from their date of arrival in the United States.

On May 12, 1975, President Gerald Ford appointed 17 persons as members of the President's Advisory Committee on Refugees to advise him and the heads of appropriate federal agencies concerning the expeditious and coordinated resettlement of Indochina refugees. To emphasize the importance of assistance to those who are in urgent need of aid for the essentials of life, the President stated:

> The people that we are welcoming today, the individuals who are in Guam or in Camp Pendleton or Eglin Air Force Base, are individuals who can contribute significantly to our society in the future. They are people of talent, they are industrious, they are individuals who want freedom and I believe they will make a contribution now and in the future to a better America.
>
> In one way or another, all of us are immigrants, and the strength of America over the years has been our diversity; diversity of all kinds of variations—religion, ethnic and otherwise. I recall very vividly a statement that seems apropos at this time, that the beauty of Joseph's coat is its many colors. The strength of America is its diversity. (Remarks of the President to the Advisory Committee on Refugees, May 13, 1975.)

The resettlement of the Vietnamese in America, despite major government efforts, has not been an easy one. Many refugees did not speak English at all upon their arrival in America. Even those who spoke English fluently were not prepared for the few scarce jobs available, due to their lack of skills. They did not know what to do or where to go.

Considerable help was provided. The private sponsors, the Red Cross, and other voluntary agencies, with the prompt action of the Congress and the Executive branch, did their best to provide shelter, food, and jobs. Public assistance programs and vocational training projects were also provided to assist during the transition. Almost four years have passed since the first Vietnamese refugees arrived in the United States. The ultimate goal of resettlement—self-sufficiency of the refugees and their integration into the American society—is in sight. Progress has been encouraging.

With the exception of the old people, most of the refugees are now employed. In contrast to the old days, the woman's role has changed dramatically. However, the old pattern of extended families remains, with most of the old people living with their children and taking care of their grandchildren.

There are several pressing problems confronting the refugees, including emotional problems for those who left spouses and children behind. There are cultural problems for the children who grow up without knowledge of ancestral customs, history and language. While most refugees are employed, because of English language difficulties or foreign degrees, jobs frequently do not fit talent, skills, and experience. Finally, because of low incomes and the need to share financial support with families in Vietnam, few can accumulate savings.

Recently, several books on Vietnam have been published in the United States. The present volume is the only one which reports upon the resettlement and adaptation of these Vietnamese to a new country, using national data. Scholars, researchers, and students badly need a volume which enables them to study the evolving role of the Vietnamese in American society. There is a need to see the progress they have made, the problems remaining to be solved, and the prospects for the future. Using current literature, government documents, and results of a study based on interviews with a national random sample of Vietnamese refugees, author Darrel Montero describes the different stages of adaptation and assimilation of the Vietnamese into a new life. Thanks to statistical evidence, the reader can follow the progress made by the refugees. The author analyzes the socioeconomic adaptation of the Vietnamese, who came from a basically agricultural region to be resettled in the most industrialized country of the world. This book provides precise details of social change experienced by the Vietnamese whose native habits, customs, and culture are so radically different from that encountered in the United States.

The reader is afforded a view of Vietnam as a nation struggling for existence throughout the centuries. Most important, the volume provides an excellent analysis of the resettlement of Vietnamese in America.

Chau Kim Nhan, who was educated at both the University of Saigon and the London School of Economics, is well known for his efforts in fighting corruption within the government of South Vietnam. His tireless efforts in seeking government reform as well as his outspokenness ultimately led to his dismissal from office by President Thieu in 1974.

# Chapter 1

# Introduction

American involvement in the war in Vietnam ended abruptly in April 1975. To a great many Americans it had been a confusing war. In the beginning there was little opposition to U.S. involvement. As the years wore on, however, opposition to the war increased. The United States first became involved in Vietnam with financial support of the French effort to halt insurgent Communists. When the French pulled out in 1954 and the country was divided along the 17th parallel, the United States became a military advisor to the government of South Vietnam. American involvment escalated as the war continued. Large numbers of American troops and dollars were enmeshed in a war which was becoming increasingly unpopular.

After a long period of diplomatic exchange, representatives of the governments of the United States and Vietnam, meeting in Paris, agreed upon a timetable for deescalating the war, exchanging prisoners, and withdrawing American troops.

In Saigon the American authorities made plans to evacuate a great number of Vietnamese when American withdrawal appeared imminent. Included in the planned evacuation were family members of United States citizens and those Vietnamese and their

1

families who were employed by the American government or businesses. Other Vietnamese who would be helped to leave were special high-risk cases, who, for various reasons, might expect their lives to be in jeopardy when the Communists took over (Hohl, 1978). As Communist troops rapidly approached Saigon in April 1975, it became apparent that the timetable for de-escalation was unworkable. The majority of Saigon residents did not realize how quickly the Communist troops were approaching the city. As the troops entered the city and American government and military personnel withdrew, relatively few of those slated to be evacuated were able to flee the country. The controlled evacuation that had been planned became instead a confused, traumatic, and, for some, a tragic event. In the final days masses of people jammed the Tan Son Nhut Airport and the United States Embassy, climbing fences, and clinging to helicopters.

In a period of one short week, thousands of Vietnamese left their country. Among the refugees were government officials who knew the war was quickly ending, members of the military who feared Communist reprisal, and masses of private citizens who fled in fear of the intense shelling (Liu and Muratta, 1977a). Those who could not get on the airplanes sometimes pushed their children on, believing they were sending them to a better life (Justus, 1976). Other Vietnamese fled by sea in small fishing boats. The fortunate ones were picked up later by friendly ships at sea, but many never were seen again. Still others fled overland through Laos and Cambodia. Those who managed to elude Communist patrols entered Thailand. These refugees were frequently suffering from disease, starvation, and exhaustion.

Temporary refugee camps were set up hastily for the Vietnamese in many Asian Pacific areas, including Thailand, Guam, Wake Island, and the Philippines. Resettling the refugees now became a task for the world community. The two nations most willing to assume responsibility for the resettlement of the Vietnamese were the United States and France (U.S., Congress, Senate, 1978:27). Small numbers of refugees were accepted by Canada, Australia, Malaysia, West Germany, Belgium, the United Kingdom, Denmark, and Austria (Table 1.1).

In a remarkably short time, the U.S. Congress found legal means to allow the refugees to enter the country. Under the Justice Department's parole authority, the refugees were able to

## TABLE 1.1

Locations of Resettlement of Indochinese Refugees, May 1975 through Dec. 1977

| Location | Total resettled | Number of boat people |
|---|---|---|
| United States | 148,355* | 3,569 |
| France | 37,353 | 1,400 |
| Canada | 6,951 | 297 |
| Australia | 4,278 | 1,199 |
| Malaysia | 1,400 | |
| West Germany | 961 | 43 |
| Belgium | 936 | 32 |
| United Kingdom | 548 | 119 |
| Denmark | 522 | |
| Austria | 223 | 22 |
| Italy | 214 | |
| Norway | 196 | 84 |
| New Zealand | 466 | 215 |
| Hong Kong | 154 | |
| Netherlands | 143 | 70 |
| Philippines | 150 | |
| Switzerland | 82 | 78 |
| Israel | 66 | 66 |
| Others | 151 | 31 |
| Total | 203,149 | 7,225 |

*Includes more than 130,000 evacuees from 1975.

Source: Adapted from U.S., Congress, Senate (1978:27).

bypass regular immigration requirements. Twelve federal agencies were directed to coordinate all necessary activities to transport and resettle the Vietnamese then in temporary refugee camps. After a brief period of processing, the refugees were flown stateside to refugee centers set up at Camp Pendleton, California; Indiantown Gap, Pennsylvania; Fort Chaffee, Arkansas; and Eglin Air Force Base, Florida. These centers operated from May until December 1975, helping the refugees to cope with problems of resettlement in a new country.

Not only did the Vietnamese suffer the trauma of being abruptly uprooted from all that was familiar, they represented a race and culture alien to a large segment of American society (Hirayama, 1977). To compound these problems, the Vietnamese refugees arrived in the United States at a time when the rate of unemployment was almost 9 percent. Many Americans feared that the refugees would take jobs from American citizens or be an added drain on the already overburdened public assistance rolls. These attitudes were reflected in a 1975 Gallup Poll that reported 54 percent of Americans felt the Vietnamese should not be permitted to stay in the United States (Kneeland, 1975).

REFUGEE DATA

Laws were necessary to provide financial, medical, and educational assistance for the new arrivals, and such legislation was quickly enacted.[1] As stipulated by the 1975 Indochina Migration and Refugee Assistance Act (PL 94-23), an Interagency Task Force composed of 12 federal agencies supervised the early stages of evacuation and resettlement. Every 90 days the task force published a series of reports assessing the problems the new immigrants faced and serving as a practical guide for federal, state, and local programs. In 1976 the U.S. Department of Health, Education, and Welfare Refugee Task Force assumed responsibility from the Interagency Task Force for overseeing domestic resettlement and publishing the reports on the status of the refugees. Since 1976 each of the HEW task force reports has included a report to Congress, an analysis of budgetary information, a list of social and rehabilitative services, and demographic data about the resettlement patterns of the refugees.[2] As of November 1978 the refugees in the United States totaled 170,698 Indochinese. Approximately 88 percent were Vietnamese, 5 percent Cambodian, and 7 percent Laotians.[3]

At the heart of the task force reports and of central interest to scholars are the data collected under the auspices of HEW in five surveys conducted from July 1975 to August 1977. These reports on the refugees provide information regarding employment, income, and public assistance of the Vietnamese refugees.

Five reports have been completed to date.[4] To a large extent these rich survey data have been overlooked by the academic community. One possible explanation for this oversight is the fact that these reports have not been published by the Government Printing Office (GPO). Rather, a limited number were reproduced and circulated internally within HEW. Because GPO does not plan to publish these reports, there is the possibility that this rich source of data may be lost to future researchers.

One of our central objectives, therefore, is to present and analyze these data for public scrutiny. The data should be easily available to scholars who may wish to further study the Vietnamese or conduct comparative studies on Cubans, Hungarians, or other recent immigrant groups. Our second objective is to develop a model of Spontaneous International Migration (SIM) in order to place the Vietnamese immigration experience in a broader sociohistorical context. While there is a growing body of literature regarding general migration patterns, Petersen (1978) recently noted the scant literature on patterns of refugee movements (Kunz, 1973). Moreover, there have been few scholarly studies on Vietnamese refugees and their adaptation to the United States.

## PROBLEMS OF STUDYING THE VIETNAMESE REFUGEES

The recency of the Vietnamese evacuation and resettlement serves as partial explanation for the paucity of literature on the refugees. In addition, the emotional exhaustion created by the war adversely affected public attitude toward the refugees. Many Americans wished to forget Vietnam and its people.

Scholars interested in the camp experience of Vietnamese refugees were hampered in their efforts by the difficulties associated with collecting systematic fieldwork data from respondents whose language and culture were different from those of the investigators themselves. Then, too, the refugee camps were in operation for a relatively short time (eight months or less), thus creating further difficulties for scholarly study. Two attempts to study the camp life of the Vietnamese refugees are of special note.

In one study, Joyce Justus (1976:76-80) notes that most studies of immigrant populations lack adequate systematic data covering the period immediately after the immigrants' arrival in the host country. Studies of Vietnamese refugees could, however, avoid the limitations of other immigrant studies which typically use data collected from immigrants long after they have arrived in their new host country. After a period of time, immigrants tend to forget or redefine many of the situations which they initially encountered. Other source material (e.g., newspaper and magazine accounts) may focus only on what the host society considers important, sensational, or significant. These accounts may not accurately reflect the immigrants' perceptions of their experiences. The Vietnamese refugees in the United States provide a

5

rare opportunity for researchers to record the experiences of a group during the earliest phase of contact with the host society.

Prior to beginning fieldwork at Camp Pendleton, Justus (1976) had anticipated conducting interviews in French. She found, however, that few Vietnamese would admit to understanding French. Those who did were either former military intelligence personnel or old persons who were unwilling to be interviewed. In addition, the Vietnamese refugees who left the camp earliest were those with the greatest language proficiency and highest socioeconomic status. Thus the character of the sample was constantly changing, thereby modifying the representativeness of the sample.

In a second paper, Stanley Wiseman (1976) also explains the problems, prospects, and pitfalls of conducting research among Vietnamese refugees at Camp Pendleton. Wiseman discusses the sampling strategies for studying what he terms "created communities," as well as problems of questionnaire construction since bilingual interviewers and interview schedules were necessary.

In an article based on participant observation and interviews, Tran Tuong Nhu (1976) describes the trauma experienced by Vietnamese refugees. The United States government policy which dispersed the Vietnamese in small groups across the land under the care of private sponsors presented a major obstacle to the Vietnamese in adjusting to American life. This policy, Tran Tuong Nhu states, separated them from their ethnic group, which they needed for comfort and emotional support.

In a study of 245 Vietnamese, Doan (1977) examines several factors which foster or impede the process of acculturation among Vietnamese refugees. The most important of these factors, Doan found, may be English language proficiency.

A monograph prepared by the U.S. Naval Health Research Unit reports on Vietnamese refugee adjustment and mental health conditions during their first 90 days at Camp Pendleton, California (Rahe, Looney, Ward, et al., 1978). Interviews were conducted with 202 refugees at the camp. In a series of four articles based on these interviews, Liu and Muratta (1977a; 1977b; 1978a; 1978b) describe the circumstances under which the Vietnamese fled their homeland and examine their resettlement in the United States. The authors compare the Vietnamese refugee camps with other relatively recent refugee settlements. The camps are assessed as to how they both hindered and helped the Vietnamese adjust to American life.

In a recent volume, Kelly (1977) provides a chronicle of the refugees' flight and immigration, as well as a brief demographic profile. The author describes the refugee camps, their social organization, cultural life, routines, and programs designed to prepare the immigrants for life in the United States. She analyzes a series of family profiles in order to determine the extent to which the Vietnamese have adjusted socially and culturally to their newly adopted country. Kelly concludes that the Vietnamese in the United States have been transformed from refugees to immigrants. These former refugees now view their future in terms of America, rather than Vietnam.

PLAN OF THE VOLUME

In this volume we examine the patterns of the refugees' socioeconomic adaptation and resettlement. As of November 1978, 170,698 Indochinese refugees were living in all of the 50 states as well as the District of Columbia, Guam, the Virgin Islands, and Puerto Rico. Table 1.2 presents a demographic breakdown of the rank order of the number of refugees in each state and possession. With nearly 47,000 refugees, California easily ranks first since Texas, in second place, has less than 16,000 refugees. Pennsylvania ranks third with approximately 8,000. At the other end of the continuum, Puerto Rico and the Virgin Islands rank last with 35 and 17 refugees, respectively.

How are the refugees coping with the obstacles which confront them? What is the financial and social status of these newly arrived refugees? What are their prospects for the future? How successful have government agencies, voluntary organizations, and private citizens been in easing the adjustment of Vietnamese refugees and aiding their resettlement in the United States?

These are the questions we seek to answer. In order to understand the Vietnamese people and the problems they face, it is useful to trace their history and the events that brought them to the United States. This is covered in Chapter Two. In Chapter Three we discuss the arrival of the Vietnamese refugees in the United States. A demographic profile of the refugees is included to identify the characteristics of those who felt impelled to leave their native land and start life anew. A look at the refugee camps,

TABLE 1.2

DISTRIBUTION OF VIETNAMESE REFUGEES IN THE UNITED STATES

| | | | | | |
|---|---|---|---|---|---|
| 1. | California | 46,637 | 28. | Nebraska | 1,456 |
| 2. | Texas | 15,894 | 29. | Tennessee | 1,386 |
| 3. | Pennsylvania | 7,642 | 30. | North Carolina | 1,277 |
| 4. | Louisiana | 7,237 | 31. | Utah | 1,275 |
| 5. | Virginia | 6,791 | 32. | Arizona | 1,244 |
| 6. | Washington | 6,104 | 33. | Alabama | 1,227 |
| 7. | Florida | 5,454 | 34. | Kentucky | 1,021 |
| 8. | Illinois | 5,210 | 35. | South Carolina | 888 |
| 9. | New York | 4,596 | 36. | Nevada | 782 |
| 10. | Minnesota | 4,160 | 37. | Mississippi | 776 |
| 11. | Oregon | 4,114 | 38. | Rhode Island | 749 |
| 12. | Oklahoma | 3,518 | 39. | New Mexico | 735 |
| 13. | Colorado | 3,464 | 40. | District of Columbia | 705 |
| 14. | Iowa | 3,055 | 41. | South Dakota | 448 |
| 15. | Missouri | 3,006 | 42. | Montana | 438 |
| 16. | Ohio | 2,994 | 43. | Idaho | 417 |
| 17. | Michigan | 2,916 | 44. | Guam | 362 |
| 18. | Maryland | 2,856 | 45. | Maine | 284 |
| 19. | Hawaii | 2,724 | 46. | North Dakota | 275 |
| 20. | Wisconsin | 2,645 | 47. | Alaska | 229 |
| 21. | Kansas | 2,185 | 48. | Delaware | 193 |
| 22. | Indiana | 1,900 | 49. | New Hampshire | 156 |
| 23. | New Jersey | 1,872 | 50. | West Virginia | 154 |
| 24. | Arkansas | 1,739 | 51. | Wyoming | 96 |
| 25. | Connecticut | 1,642 | 52. | Vermont | 52 |
| 26. | Georgia | 1,607 | 53. | Puerto Rico | 35 |
| 27. | Massachusetts | 1,582 | 54. | Virgin Islands | 17 |
| | | | 55. | State Unknown | 477 |
| | | | | TOTAL | 170,698 |

Source: These data are compiled from Immigration and Naturalization Service statistics and HEW estimates as of November 1, 1978. These latest figures were obtained from a personal communication with Edward Sponga, Special Programs Division, Office of Family Assistance, Social Security Administration, December 13, 1978.

voluntary agencies, and sponsors provides one basis for assessing the refugees' adaptation to American life.

In Chapter Four we analyze the results of five sample surveys based upon a population of some 35,000 refugees. We trace the changing socioeconomic status of the Vietnamese in America over a period of two years and examine the current circumstances under which the Vietnamese live. In Chapter Five, drawing upon available data, we construct a sociohistorical model of the Vietnamese migration experience. The model attempts to predict the prospects for future socioeconomic adaptation and cultural assimilation of the Vietnamese.

Chapter Six summarizes our central findings and discusses the continuing influx of refugees from Indochina. We examine the status of research on the Vietnamese and present an agenda for future research.

## NOTES

1. For a detailed chronology of the events surrounding the American withdrawal from Vietnam and subsequent legislation, see Appendix A.

2. See U.S. Department of State, Interagency Task Force on Indochina Refugees. *Report to the Congress:* Dated June 15, 1975; September 15, 1975; December 15, 1975; and U.S. Department of Health, Education, and Welfare (HEW) Refugee Task Force. *Report to the Congress:* Dated March 15, 1976; June 15, 1976; September 20, 1976; December 20, 1976; March 21, 1977; June 20, 1977; September 21, 1977; December 31, 1977.

3. These data are compiled from Immigration and Naturalization Service statistics and HEW estimates. These latest figures were obtained from a personal communication with Edward Sponga, Special Programs Division, Office of Family Assistance, Social Security Administration, December 13, 1978.

4. See the following five reports: Opportunity Systems, Inc. *First Wave Report, Vietnam Resettlement Operational Feedback.* Contract No. HEW-100-76-0042. Washington, D.C., October 2, 1975; Opportunity Systems, Inc. *Second Wave Report, Vietnam Resettlement Operational Feedback.* Washington, D.C., January, 1976; Opportunity Systems, Inc. *Third Wave Report, Vietnam Resettlement Operational Feedback.* Washington, D.C. September, 1976; Opportunity Systems, Inc. *Fourth Wave Report, Vietnam Resettlement Operational Feedback.* Washington, D.C., September, 1977; Opportunity Systems, Inc. *Fifth Wave Report, Vietnam Resettlement Operational Feedback.* Washington, D.C., October, 1977.

# Chapter 2

# Vietnam: A History in Brief

Any attempt to understand Vietnamese refugees and their current status should start with a history of the nation and its people. While one short chapter cannot do justice to the history of a nation as old and culturally rich as that of Vietnam, we shall attempt a summary in order to gain a broader perspective for understanding the motivations and desires of the Vietnamese who fled.

Vietnam is a small nation in Southeast Asia, located on what is termed the Indochina Peninsula. While Vietnam has adopted many of the cultural characteristics of the larger nations of India and China, it nevertheless has maintained a culture distinctly its own throughout many centuries of outside influence and, at times, domination. Vietnam was originally a heterogeneous mixture of varying racial and cultural types. The diverse groups of which her population is composed have succeeded in retaining through the years their own variations of language, religion, and customs. This rich mixture has created a cultural pattern unique to the nation of Vietnam.

## PREHISTORY

The very earliest history of Vietnam is a combination of legend and folklore passed orally from generation to generation. The original inhabitants of Vietnam are thought to be Austro-Negroid migrants. They were followed by an influx of migratory Mongolian tribes who, in turn, were pushed southward by the Chinese (Bain, 1967). The earliest known kingdom of Vietnam, Van Lang, came into existence sometime between 1000 and 500 B.C. It was conquered by an aggressor from the north who founded Au Lac, a short-lived kingdom which existed for only 50 years. Little is known about these kingdoms, which are mentioned only in folklore (Hall, 1955). The kingdom of Au Lac was subjugated in 207 B.C. by a Chinese general who founded the independent state of Nam Viet (Buttinger, 1968). It is at this point that the authenticated history of the country known to us as Vietnam begins.

## 1000 YEARS OF CHINESE RULE

For almost 100 years the tiny nation of Nam Viet held out against the ever-expanding Chinese Empire. When the Chinese, after many years of internal strife, united under the Han dynasty, Nam Viet was finally conquered and colonized in 111 B.C. (Grousset, 1953).

China ruled Vietnam for 1,000 years. During that time the Vietnamese adopted Chinese clothing, customs, and forms of government (Bain, 1967). Yet the Chinese failed to assimilate the people of this tiny nation, who exhibited remarkable ethnic durability and tenacity, adhering to their own language and unique culture. The long prehistory of the Vietnamese had given them a sense of their own identity. Despite their location at the edge of the Chinese empire, they were able to ignore Chinese attempts at domination because China was often distracted during times of internal strife or war (Buttinger, 1968).

The conquered Vietnamese suffered under their often brutal Chinese overlords. Though Vietnam grew rich, experiencing technological and economic progress under Chinese rule, the bulk of its population remained poor. The peasants were forced to contribute labor, taxes, and recruits for the army. The old Vietnamese feudal lords also resented the Chinese, who had usurped their positions of power and authority.

The Vietnamese launched numerous rebellions against Chinese rule over the years, but the uprisings had little tangible effect. Primarily the revolts were upper-class affairs in which the large masses of common people played but a small part. The revolts failed for that reason. Eventually, however, even the most aristocratic of revolutionaries realized that the peasants were a valuable source of nationalistic spirit and came to view them as allies. This lesson was not forgotten by the modern revolutionaries in Vietnam. As the upper-class Vietnamese wooed the peasants and appealed to their common interests, successful revolution became a possibility. The passive resistance of the peasants over the years probably did more to throw off Chinese rule than all the upper-class armed rebellions (Buttinger, 1968).

## 900 YEARS OF INDEPENDENCE

Seizing the opportunity of a China weakened by internal strife, the Vietnamese drove the Chinese armies out of their country in 939 A.D. Over the next 900 years Vietnam maintained its independence through the tactic of alternately paying tributes to China and repelling successfully a series of attempted invasions. Included were two attempts by Kublai Khan in 1284 and 1287 (Bain, 1967; Buttinger, 1968). During this period the Vietnamese expanded further southward into the Indochina Peninsula, colonizing the lower Mekong Delta.

Independence was interrupted by one brief period of Chinese rule when the Chinese army under the Ming dynasty invaded Vietnam in 1406 and remained in control for ten years. The cruel treatment the Vietnamese received from the Chinese during those ten years led to a burning hatred of the Chinese and a resurgence of Vietnamese national pride. A ten-year war, led by the courageous hero, Le Loi, pushed the Chinese from Vietnam once more. Le Loi, who was a pioneer in the use of guerrilla warfare, became the founder of the Le dynasty.

Referred to as Vietnam's "architect of national unity," Le Loi instituted agricultural reforms and redistribution of land (Buttinger, 1968). Once again, however, the peasants were the last to be considered. As land was doled out first to influential upper-class Vietnamese and military officers, there was none left over for the lower Vietnamese classes. Powerful overlords emerged, subjugating the peasants and squabbling among them-

13

selves. They split the country as no outside force had been able to do, ushering in 150 years of struggle between two powerful feudal families, the Trinh in the North and the Nguyen in the South. During those years of strife, the peasants alone, bound together by the strong culture of village life, preserved the national unity of Vietnam.

Finally, in the year 1772 a rebellion started which had the support of the peasants and middle-class merchants. Known as the Tay Son rebellion, it was named after three brothers who led the revolt to overthrow both the Nguyen and the Trinh. By 1787 these three brothers had complete control of the nation. Their rule was brief, but the unification of Vietnam survived their downfall in 1802. The man most responsible for the demise of the Tay Son regime was Nguyen Anh, the only survivor of the powerful family which had once ruled the South. He founded the last Vietnamese dynasty, the Nguyen, which remained in power until October 1955, when Emperor and Chief of State Bao Dai was dismissed (Buttinger, 1958; 1968).

## Europeans Discover Vietnam

In order to understand why Europeans eventually dominated Vietnam, it is necessary to backtrack to the year 1535 when the Portuguese arrived in Vietnam. The sixteenth century was the zenith of Portugal's maritime greatness. Portugal dominated Asian waters, effectively controlling all Western trade with Vietnam and holding off all competitors. By the papal decree of 1493, which divided the known world between Spain and Portugal to Christianize, Vietnam had become the responsibility of Portugal. In the name of Christianity Portugal often seized upon economic opportunity. Merchants arrived with missionaries, and for 100 years the Portuguese maintained exclusive control of Vietnamese trade until challenged by the arrival of the Dutch in 1636.

Because the Portuguese were hostile to Dutch efforts in the South, the Dutch concentrated their efforts in the North. There they established a trading post with the support of the powerful Trinh family. In 1672 the English opened a trading office, but their commercial efforts were blocked by both the Dutch and Portuguese. English efforts were never successful in Vietnam. The French also opened a trading office in 1680, but by that time

14

Vietnamese trade was no longer profitable for European entrepreneurs.

The Western nations were not able to plunder Vietnam as they did other Asian countries during the 17th Century. In fact, European influence might have ended in Vietnam by 1700 because trade in that country simply was not profitable for the Europeans. Under the Trinhs and Nguyens, Vietnam had a government stronger than most other Asian countries of that time, and in many respects it was able to handle outside threats. English and Dutch traders faded out of the picture, leaving only the French and Portuguese as ambassadors of European influence. These merchants too might have left in a short time, but the Catholic Church was not so easily discouraged. The church still sought converts, and with the English and Dutch gone, French and Portuguese missionaries stepped up their proselytyzing efforts.

As missionaries, the French had gained dominance in Vietnam through the efforts of a French churchman, Monsignor Alexander of Rhodes. In the face of solid opposition from both the Nguyens and Trinhs, who feared that Catholicism might weaken the peasants' allegiance to their overlords, Rhodes sought more active support from Portuguese missionaries. Failing in this, he turned to Rome for support of a plan which would free his missionaries from Portuguese control. Rebuffed by the Vatican, Rhodes appealed to his native France and was successful in enlisting the support of the French church. The Society of Foreign Missions, founded in Paris in 1664, became the major arm of Christian influence in Vietnam. Repeating a familiar cycle, the interests of merchants and missionaries were soon allied once again.

Years of struggle followed, and at one point foreign Christian missionaries were expelled by the Vietnamese government. The missionaries were viewed with suspicion by the Vietnamese government, which considered them to be agents of a foreign power. A long ban on the Christian religion ended when the French Bishop of Adran, Pigneau de Béhaine, saved the life of the 16-year-old nephew of the Nguyen king. This occurred during the Tay Son rebellion in 1777. Pigneau then pressed the French court to expand its influence in Indochina. When the Nguyens defeated the Tay Sons and returned to power in 1802, they continued to look upon France with some measure of respect.

However, a new wave of European aggression was directed toward Asia in the early 1800's, causing the Nguyen rulers to react with suspicion and hostility towards the West. Christian missionaries once again were looked upon as subversive agents and faced death or expulsion. Western interest in Vietnam continued to increase, however, and when Emperor Tu Duc died in 1883, France quickly moved in to claim Vietnam as a colony (Buttinger, 1968).

## THE FRENCH IN VIETNAM

The fall of Vietnam to France was part of a larger struggle between the French and the British to seize chunks of Asia for economic exploitation. In the early 1800's France had tried through peaceful and diplomatic methods to obtain trading privileges in Vietnam, but these efforts had failed. The French then had no contacts at all with Vietnam for decades, with the exception of the missionaries who continued their efforts to turn the people to Christianity. During those years, however, the anti-Catholic policy of the Nguyen regime made martyrs of the Christians in Vietnam and provided France with an excuse for military intervention in Vietnam.

The missionaries, ignoring their own immediate peril, pressured France under Napoleon to subdue the Nguyen regime by force. For the next 30 years the French pushed ahead with a piecemeal military conquest of Vietnam. Tu Duc, the last emperor of independent Vietnam, died in July 1883. On August 25, 1883, a Treaty of Protectorate was signed with France, making Vietnam a French colony (Buttinger, 1968). The conquest of Vietnam occurred, not because the French government or French people as a whole demanded it, but because certain Frenchmen wanted to promote their own financial and religious interests.

Conquest by France was humiliating to a people who had repelled 15 invasions by China. Contrary to French propaganda at home, the French were not welcomed by the Vietnamese government or people. From the very beginning of French rule, the Vietnamese sought revenge and made plans to regain their independence. Finding chaos everywhere and receiving no cooperation from the Vietnamese, France's immediate goal was to establish a strong central administration within the colony. Local mandarins were replaced with young, inexperienced French officers. Individual Frenchmen came to Indochina seeking government employment and wealth, and French private enterprise flourished.

Periods of crises punctuated the French rule. Necessary reforms were neglected as a succession of governors applied their own programs and methods. Paul Doumer, appointed governor in 1896, was among the most notable. It was Doumer who was most responsible for turning Vietnam into France's richest colony, typically at the expense of the native populace. In a misguided effort to westernize Vietnam, he initiated a program of building numerous railroads, bridges, and harbors. The only persons who truly benefited from this building program were the businessmen in the companies that did the construction. The only programs to prove worthwhile to the Vietnamese, giving them lasting benefit, were the newly built harbors and a variety of agricultural improvements (Buttinger, 1968). Also, the establishment of *l'Ecole Francaise d'Extrême Orient,* a scientific institute, proved to be a valuable French contribution.

To finance the unproductive public works programs, the French instituted a most unjust system of colonial taxation: the Vietnamese paid dearly, but the French, who grew rich, paid nothing. This tax system, coupled with the swelling ranks of political prisoners and the often brutal treatment of the native populace, did not enhance the French image in the eyes of the Vietnamese people. As one governor after another remained ignorant of the social and political consequences of French colonial policy, a series of secret Vietnamese associations were formed for the express purpose of throwing off French rule.

In France a few well-informed critics began to denounce French policy in Indochina. For the most part, however, the French government and people remained indifferent to colonial affairs. In Vietnam a governor now and then appeared on the scene who was sincerely interested in making life better for the Vietnamese and who wanted to promote good relations between the French and the local inhabitants. But such efforts were essentially too little, too late, and were always undermined by the basic inequities of colonialism itself.

As the Vietnamese became ever more determined to rid themselves of French rule, two rival nationalist movements emerged with fundamental differences in ideologies and methods. One followed the path of Western individualism, and the other adhered

17

to Communist doctrine. The Communists, led by Ho Chi Minh, gained ascendance in the nationalist movement because of their superior organization, their use of deception when expedient, and the murder of opposition nationalist leaders (Bain, 1967). During World War II, when Japan occupied parts of Vietnam, Ho Chi Minh seized the opportunity to form the Vietnam Independence League (the Vietminh) and started an insurrection against the French. Just two weeks after VJ Day, on August 29, 1945, Vietnam became a unified country under Ho Chi Minh known as the Democratic Republic of Vietnam.

## WAR IN VIETNAM

The French, however, prepared to return to Vietnam at the end of the war, completely convinced of their right to be there and blind to the political realities of the day. Through a combination of military and political errors, the French never achieved complete control of Vietnam after World War II, and eventually France lost the colony entirely. On March 6, 1946, France signed an agreement with the Vietminh, recognizing it as the only legitimate native political regime for all of Vietnam. At the same time France obtained the right to move troops into the North. Several months later the two parties met again in Paris at the Fontainebleau conference (Buttinger, 1958). This meeting was intended to provide some basis for further agreement between the French and Vietnamese, but their differences were irreconcilable and the conference broke up.

By now Ho Chi Minh had great prestige in Vietnam for having formed a quasi-government under the noses of the French. In October 1946, the government of Ho Chi Minh formed an army headed by General Vo Nguyen Giap and war appeared imminent. A month later at the harbor of Haiphong a battle between the Vietminh and the French marked the beginning of the French-Indochina War, which was to last until 1954. For much of the world it was a confusing war. On the one hand, the war appeared to be a duel between communism and democracy. On the other hand, it was a struggle between nationalism and colonialism. Support for the independence of Vietnam was often construed as support of communism. On May 28, 1947, the Front of National Union was founded in Saigon in response to this dilemma. Composed of anti-Communist moderates, the Front was led

18

by Social Democrat Nguyen Van Sam, who was later assassinated by the Communists (Devillers, 1953).

The Communists, however, under Ho Chi Minh, gained recognition for their Democratic Republic of Vietnam from the newly victorious Communist party in China on January 16, 1950. On January 31, the Communist government in Moscow also extended official recognition to Ho's government.

Fearing that all of Asia would fall to the Communists after the takeover in North Korea, the United States began to supply aid to the French in Indochina. After the Korean Armistice in 1953, the United States increased its aid to the French, but it was too late. With the fall of Dien Bien Phu in 1954, the French were defeated.

The Geneva Agreements of 1954 ended the eight-year struggle by the French to reassert their colonial rule in Vietnam. Vietnam had won her independence but lost her unity. The agreements divided Vietnam along the 17th parallel. The north was given to the Communists under Ho Chi Minh, and the South was to be led by an anti-Communist government under Premier Ngo Dinh Diem. A prominent nationalist, Diem had been unable to support either the French or the Vietminh and had left the country in 1950. France now supported Diem as a compromise candidate in an effort to keep the entire nation from falling to the communists. Diem was not a charismatic leader and was mistrusted by all factions: the French, the Communists, and the Nationalists. He was swept into office by the tide of events but lacked mass support and was opposed openly by the police and the army.

The governments of both North and South Vietnam each claimed to be the only legitimate government of Vietnam. According to the Geneva Agreements, Vietnam was to be reunited by national elections in 1956. These elections were never held, however, because conditions never existed which would have allowed true freedom of choice.

After the 1954 Agreements were signed, the governments of North and South Vietnam consolidated their positions. The North greatly increased its number of military units and used force to block the flow of refugees south. At the same time the Communists forced thousands of youths north across the 17th parallel and began a reign of terror against the traditional Vietnamese

19

village and provincial leadership. Southern Communists, known as the Vietcong, launched an uprising in the South on a slowly accelerating scale so as to avoid undue international attention (U.S., Congress, Senate, 1955).

The domino theory, which dominated U.S. foreign policy for 20 years, held that if one small country such as Vietnam fell to the Communists, the neighboring countries would fall in rapid succession. The ultimate effect would be world domination by the Communists. On that premise the United States provided large-scale economic aid to the Diem government and sent military advisors and equipment to South Vietnam. Between 1960 and 1962 the Communists upgraded their struggle into a "war of liberation." They established a political arm in South Vietnam consisting of the National Liberation Front and the Peoples' Revolutionary Party. Whole battalions and divisions of the North Vietnamese army moved south to join the Vietcong in guerrilla warfare.

As the Communist efforts increased, the Diem regime became ever more restrictive, losing what little support it enjoyed. After militant Buddhist demonstrations, the army overthrew Diem in 1963, and the country was then ruled by a series of military and civilian governments. Military assistance from the United States continued to increase to match the Communist escalation and by 1966 amounted to full-scale military involvement (Bain, 1967). The United States had now replaced the French as the target and rallying point for Vietnamese Communists.

Fearful of international reaction and possible retaliation by the Chinese or Russians, the United States declined to invade North Vietnam. Instead, the United States became mired in a frustrating holding pattern while attempts were made to bolster the political leaders and army of South Vietnam until that country could gain enough popular support to win the war itself. In the United States the war was becoming increasingly unpopular. Antiwar activists and protestors led mass demonstrations and gained much support.

The war finally ended in April 1975 with the fall of Saigon to North Vietnamese troops. In the panic that ensued, thousands of Vietnamese fled the country seeking safety and refuge in the United States and other countries. Chapter Three begins the story of these refugees.

20

# Chapter 3

# The Arrival of the Vietnamese Refugees

It is natural at this point to want to know more about those Vietnamese who endured the dangers of fleeing their native country for an uncertain future in a strange land. One objective of this chapter, therefore, is to lay out the parameters of the demographic characteristics of the Vietnamese refugees. These data are based upon the total population of all Vietnamese refugees in the United States for which data presently are available. These data should be distinguished from those we report in Chapter Four which are based upon a systematic random sample of Vietnamese resettled throughout the United States. After examining the demographic characteristics of the Vietnamese who fled to America, we turn to a discussion of the process by which the Vietnamese were resettled in the United States and the problems which they encountered as a result of that resettlement.

## DEMOGRAPHIC PROFILE

*Sex and Age.* Data collected by the Immigration and Naturalization Service based on 114,140 Alien Address Reports provide information regarding the sex and age distribution of Indo-

21

china refugees.[1] The refugees are almost equally divided between males and females (51 percent and 49 percent respectively). The Vietnamese refugees are a relatively young population with 43 percent being children aged 17 and under (Table 3.1). More than one in three (37 percent) are between the ages of 18 and 34. Only 7 percent fall between 45 and 62 years of age, and less than 5 percent are 63 or older (U.S. Department of HEW, 1976b:25).

*Education and Income.* The Vietnamese refugees are relatively well-educated by any standard, and in South Vietnam they were, for the most part, among the educated elite. Based on a sample of 124,457 respondents, nearly fifty percent of the heads of household have at least a secondary school education, and more than 25 percent are college and university graduates (U.S. Department of State, 1975c:12). Information is not available on the income status of the refugees before they left Vietnam. However, the unusually high level of educational attainment within this group indicates that many of the refugees were among the financially well-to-do in Vietnam (Kelly, 1977).

TABLE 3.1

AGE AND SEX DISTRIBUTION OF REFUGEE POPULATION

| AGE | MALE | | FEMALE | | TOTAL | |
|---|---|---|---|---|---|---|
| 0 - 5 | 8,250 | 14.24% | 8,319 | 14.80% | 16,569 | 14.52% |
| 6 - 11 | 8,485 | 14.65 | 8,269 | 14.71 | 16,754 | 14.68 |
| 12 - 17 | 7,824 | 13.51 | 7,487 | 13.32 | 15,311 | 13.41 |
| 18 - 24 | 11,364 | 19.62 | 9,476 | 16.85 | 20,840 | 18.26 |
| 25 - 34 | 10,612 | 18.32 | 10,212 | 18.16 | 20,824 | 18.25 |
| 35 - 44 | 5,481 | 9.46 | 5,115 | 9.10 | 10,596 | 9.28 |
| 45 - 62 | 4,046 | 6.99 | 4,175 | 7.43 | 8,221 | 7.20 |
| 63 + | 1,857 | 3.21 | 3,168 | 5.63 | 5,025 | 4.40 |
| TOTAL | 57.919 | 100.00% | 56.221 | 100.00% | 114,140 | 100.00% |

Source: Adapted from the U.S. Department of Health, Education, and Welfare (1976b:25).

*Occupation.* The data available on overall job categories occupied in Vietnam indicate that the refugees have a broad spectrum of occupational skills. Among the heads of household a plurality (24 percent) have professional, technical, or managerial skills. The next largest category, 16.9 percent, name transportation, and 11.7 percent have clerical and sales expertise. Only 4.9 percent list skills as farmers or fishermen (U.S. Department of State, 1975c:13). It is not known how many of the refugees are former military personnel or government officials. These persons may be included under professional, technical, and managerial occupations, or they may be among those 7.9 percent who did not report their former occupation. (See Table 3.2.)

TABLE 3.2

PRIMARY EMPLOYMENT SKILLS OF HEADS OF HOUSEHOLDS*

| | | |
|---|---|---|
| Medical Professions | 2,210 | 7.2% |
| Professional, technical & managerial | 7,368 | 24.0 |
| Clerical and sales | 3,572 | 11.7 |
| Service | 2,324 | 7.6 |
| Farming, fishing, forestry | 1,491 | 4.9 |
| Agricultural processing | 128 | 0.4 |
| Machine trades | 2,670 | 8.7 |
| Benchwork, assembly & repair | 1,249 | 4.1 |
| Structural and construction | 2,026 | 6.6 |
| Transportation and miscellaneous | 5,165 | 16.9 |
| Not reported | 2,425 | 7.9 |
| TOTAL | 30,628 | 100.0% |

* Based on a sample of 124,457
Source: Adapted from U.S. Department of State (1975c:13).

*Urban-rural Background.* Looking at the statistics on educational attainment, we can arrive at some tentative conclusions as to the background of the refugees. Secondary schools and universities in Vietnam are concentrated in the larger cities. Given the high level of educational attainment of the heads of household, we suspect that a great many of the refugees have urban rather than rural backgrounds. Interviews conducted at Camp Pendleton, California, appear to substantiate this conjecture. The findings indicate that only 25 percent of those interviewed came from rural settings (Rahe, Looney, Ward, et al., 1978).

*Household Size and Composition.* There are cultural differences in the way in which Americans and Vietnamese view the extended family. Whereas Americans tend to focus on the nuclear family (mother, father, and children), Vietnamese are apt to consider a much larger circle of relatives as constituting their family household. Grandparents, uncles, aunts, cousins—all are united in strong ties of kinship and loyalty.

Data collected by the U.S. Immigration and Naturalization Service reveal that the number of extended family groups who were able to flee Vietnam together is remarkably high. Based on a sample of 124,493 respondents, approximately 62 percent of all immigrants arrived in family groups of five or more. Although the average household size is 3.3 persons, this figure is misleading because it includes one-person families (U.S. Department of Health, Education, and Welfare, 1976b:27). Perhaps a more accurate picture is provided by sample surveys conducted at the resettlement camps. For instance, at Fort Indiantown Gap, Pennsylvania, the average number of children per refugee family is four. This figure is high by American standards, but in Vietnam the average family has six children. Considering the circumstances of their immigration, it is remarkable that so many large families were able to flee together. Among those interviewed at Fort Indiantown Gap, the largest refugee families tend to be those from the rural areas of Vietnam (Kelly, 1977).

*Religion.* We must rely on sample surveys conducted at resettlement camps in order to draw some conclusions about the entire refugee population given that the Task Force Reports do not include data on religious preferences. Interviews conducted at Camp Pendleton reveal that 55 percent of the refugees are Roman Catholics and 27 percent are Buddhists (Rahe, Looney, Ward, et al., 1978). A study at Fort Indiantown Gap reveals similar results. Over 40 percent of the refugees report that they are Catholic (Kelly, 1977). Thus, Catholics, who constitute less than 10 percent of the population in Vietnam, appear to be disproportionately overrepresented among the Vietnamese refugees.

THE REFUGEE CAMPS

The first of the four refugee camps to open was Camp Pendleton, California on April 29, 1975. Fort Chaffee, Arkansas quickly followed, opening May 2. Then came Eglin Air Force Base, Florida, May 4, and Fort Indiantown Gap, Pennsylvania, May 28. Set up as relocation centers, they became temporary homes to tens of thousands of Indochinese refugees awaiting job offers and resettlement.

The camps were run jointly by the Interagency Task Force (IATF) and the U.S. military, whose responsibilities and goals often overlapped and conflicted. The military (the Marines at Camp Pendleton, the Air Force at Eglin, and the Army at Forts Chaffee and Indiantown Gap) was officially in charge of security and logistics, including food service and basic supplies for the refugees. The IATF, whose personnel came from 12 different government agencies, was in charge of providing cultural programs, implementing government policy, and the processing and resettlement of the refugees (U.S. Department of State, 1975b). The Interagency Task Force in Washington established overall government policy toward the Vietnamese.

As soon as possible after their arrival at the camps, the refugees were interviewed and screened for security purposes. They were given physical examinations, identification numbers, and were registered with the voluntary agencies that would be responsible for their resettlement. Families were housed in small quarters within tents or barracks, which provided very little privacy or security from theft. Much of the refugee's day was taken up by standing in line waiting to be fed or interviewed (Liu and Muratta, 1978a).

Organizations such as the Red Cross and the YMCA offered a variety of social services. They provided child-care classes, college placement services, and recreational programs (Kelly, 1977). Table tennis, television, movies, and newspapers were available on a regular basis. Orientation meetings were held regularly in a diligent effort to help the Vietnamese learn about their new country. While in camp, children attended school and adults could take classes focusing on vocational skills and English language training. A study of refugees at Camp Pendleton revealed that the average Vietnamese spent four hours daily studying the English language. Fully 70 percent of the refugee population at Camp Pendleton took part in the English language program (Liu and Muratta, 1978a).

## The Role of the Voluntary Agencies

Once the refugees had been interviewed, given a medical examination, and assigned to living quarters within the camp, they were quickly assigned to one of the nine voluntary agencies (VOLAGs) which assumed the task of finding sponsors for the refugees and resettling them in the mainstream of American society. These agencies included the United States Catholic Conference (USCC), the Lutheran Immigration and Refugee Service (LIRS), the International Rescue Committee (IRC), United HIAS, Church World Service (CWS), the Tolstoy Foundation, the American Fund for Czechoslovak Refugees (AFCR), the American Council for Nationalities Services (ACNS), and Travelers' Aid-International Social Services (U.S. Department of Health, Education, and Welfare, 1977d).

The personnel within these nongovernmental voluntary agencies had diverse social and professional backgrounds. Many were professional social workers, some had a religious orientation, while others were secular workers who had worked in Vietnam. Several, in fact, spoke Vietnamese. Other agencies were composed mainly of nonprofessional personnel, who had themselves been immigrants to the United States from countries other than Vietnam.

The VOLAGs were under contract to the Interagency Task Force to find individual or group sponsors who would assume fiscal and personal responsibility for the refugee families for a period of up to two years. To that end, the IATF gave the agencies a sum of $500 per refugee as a resettlement grant, which each agency could allocate as it saw fit (Kelly, 1977).

The IATF personnel were administrators whose goals were to get the refugees resettled as quickly as possible. This created some conflict with VOLAG personnel who were more inclined to screen prospective sponsors very carefully and move more slowly in an effort to make resettlement for the Vietnamese as painless as possible (Kelly, 1977). The IATF established a 45-day limit for the agencies to assign refugees to sponsors and move them out of camp (U.S. Department of State, 1975b). This tight deadline upset VOLAG personnel, but for the most part they were compelled to go along with it, and the refugees were rapidly moved in and out of the camps.

SPONSORSHIP AND RESETTLEMENT

There were only four ways for the refugees to leave the camps: (1) obtain permission for third-country resettlement

26

through the embassy of that country; (2) seek repatriation to Vietnam; (3) offer proof of enough financial reserves to be self-supporting; or (4) find an American individual or group willing to act as a sponsor (Kelly, 1977).

Third-country resettlement was greatly encouraged by the U.S. government. Facilities were provided for other countries to set up offices at the camps to recruit refugees. Camp newspapers ran articles encouraging resettlement elsewhere. As it turned out, however, resettlement in a third country was not a major option for the Vietnamese, mainly because other countries were not willing to grant blanket acceptance to the refugees. They preferred to take the cream of the crop and often would accept only badly needed professionals (such as doctors and dentists), those with relatives in that country, or those who could speak the language of the prospective host country (Kelly, 1977).

A small number of refugees sought to return to Vietnam. By October 1975, repatriation had been granted to 1,546 refugees by the new government of Vietnam. In general, these repatriates were military personnel assigned to ships or airplanes whose commanders had decided to flee Vietnam. Typically, these men had been forced to leave their wives and families behind. Since that time at least 400 more Vietnamese have expressed the desire to be repatriated, but the Vietnamese government thus far has been unwilling to accept them (U.S. Department of Health, Education, and Welfare, 1976a).

To be considered financially self-supporting, the Task Force required a refugee family to show proof of cash reserves totalling at least $4000 per household member. Obviously this option was closed to all but a fortunate few: the great majority of Vietnamese were forced to wait for sponsors who would usher them into American life.

Sponsorship of a refugee family entailed a substantial financial obligation. The sponsors were to provide food, clothing, and shelter until the Vietnamese became self-supporting. They were to assist the refugees in finding employment, enrolling their children in schools, and understanding American customs. Initially, sponsors were also expected to assume financial responsibility for the refugees' health care, except in the case of unemployed Vietnamese who were helped to some extent by Medicare (Kelly, 1977).

One agency estimated the average cost to resettle a Vietnamese family to be a minimum of $5,601 (U.S., Congress, Senate, 1975). Sponsors usually received part of the $500 grant given the VOLAGs for resettling each refugee, but never was the amount nearly enough to compensate them for the expenses incurred. Thus, very few individuals could afford to act as sponsors, and group sponsorships became the norm.

Employment opportunities became the major focus of the resettlement effort. Sometimes U.S. corporations which had formerly employed the refugees in Vietnam acted as their sponsors when they arrived in the United States. Other companies seemed to welcome the opportunity to hire cheap labor.

A few of the refugees had relatives already living in the United States. In such cases these relatives acted as sponsors. Some sponsorships were arranged through the Catholic Church and its Vietnamese clergy, many of whom were in the United States prior to the arrival of the refugees. The voluntary agencies which were church-affiliated preferred to assign the refugees to local congregations as their sponsors. It was their view that individual sponsorship put too much pressure, both financial and emotional, on the sponsor, and corporation sponsorships offered too much potential for exploitation of the refugees.

In many ways the sponsorship program contributed to the dispersal of the Vietnamese across America. Because few individuals could afford to act as sponsors and the number of organizations willing to act as sponsors within a given community was limited, the Vietnamese were scattered across the country by their assignment to sponsors. In addition, the influx of refugees took place during a time of economic recession in the United States. It seemed unwise to encourage large numbers of refugees to descend on a single area, creating a visible drain on diminishing job markets and thus inviting the hostility of the local residents.

At first the refugees could refuse to accept the sponsors which had been selected for them, and they often did so. Reasons given for rejecting sponsors varied from a dislike of cold weather in the northern states to a fear of encountering racial prejudice, fear of isolation from other Vietnamese, or fear of exploitation. Some of the fears expressed by the Vietnamese were well founded. Other refugees were reluctant to leave the security of camp life to face an uncertain future.

In the camps, class distinctions were quite apparent among the refugees. The wealthier refugees did not eat at the chow lines. They had staff members purchase food and clothing for them outside the camp. These refugees were among the first to leave the camps. The less affluent fishermen and farmers were easily identified: their dress was different from the rest, they could not speak English, and they were hesitant to deal with the resettlement agencies. Despised by the upper classes because they did not appear to want to leave camp, they were nevertheless dependent on their more affluent English-speaking countrymen who felt little sympathy for them (Justus, 1976).

As resettlement efforts moved from the easy to place refugees to those who proved more difficult, placements became increasingly arbitrary. Agencies which appeared to be taking too much time to match refugees and sponsors were, in effect, threatened by the 45-day limit to resettle refugees. If refugees were not resettled during that time, the Task Force would remove them from an agency's list and ask state and local agencies to assume the task. These state and local agencies actually resettled only a small number of refugees, but they played an important part in speeding up the work of the VOLAGs, who looked with some disdain upon the resettlement methods employed by the local agencies.

The participation of the Vietnamese in their own resettlement was always minimal, but this was especially true toward the closing dates of the camps. In an effort to close the camps and resettle the refugees as quickly and economically as possible, Task Force policy, in effect, pushed the Vietnamese out of camps and into sometimes inappropriate sponsorship situations. It was Task Force policy that was responsible for scattering the Vietnamese across the land. It was the Task Force that set the closing dates for the camps and pressured the voluntary agencies into speeding up the resettlement process. It can also be argued that it was the Task Force that efficiently moved thousands of Vietnamese into the mainstream of American life, in a manner which created the smallest possible financial burden for American taxpayers, who already viewed the refugees with some degree of hostility.

As noted earlier, most of the refugees are young; nearly half are Catholic; most come from urban settings and relatively well-to-do families; and many are among Vietnam's educational elite who occupied a relatively high social and economic status in

Vietnam. These background characteristics would appear to bode well for the successful adjustment of the Vietnamese refugees to American society. However, considering the extraordinary circumstances in which the refugees left Vietnam, the rapidity with which they were dispatched from the camps to make their own way, and the sometimes hostile reaction they encountered, it is understandable that the refugees would have encountered some problems in resettlement.

## PROBLEMS OF RESETTLEMENT

*Psychological Preparation.* Although many refugees at one time worked for Americans in well-paying jobs, the rest were less accustomed to Western culture. Regardless of their background, few refugees were prepared for life in the United States. The abruptness of the evacuation left most refugees psychologically unprepared to start life anew. They had made no calculated decision to emigrate but had fled what seemed an untenable situation. In a survey conducted at Camp Pendleton in the summer of 1975, 73 percent of those interviewed said they felt they had no alternative but to leave Vietnam. Nevertheless, half of the refugees interviewed expressed some regret at having left family, fortune, and homeland (Liu and Muratta, 1977a).

*Ethnic Community and the Family.* The Vietnamese refugees faced serious language and cultural barriers and, unlike most other recent immigrants, they found no indigenous ethnic community to offer them support. Any inclinations they may have had to form such an ethnic community were not facilitated by the U.S. government policy of spreading them across the country as quickly as possible. Moreover, the Vietnamese were greatly distressed by the separation of extended families. Many had left relatives behind in Vietnam, and other family groups became separated and emigrated to different countries. Family reunion problems contributed greatly to the refugees' anguish and threatened to inhibit their adjustment to life in the United States (U.S., Congress, Senate, 1978).

*Economic Self-sufficiency.* The jobs open to the refugees in this country were for the most part lower level, offering low pay and little opportunity for advancement. This has caused an emotional crisis of some proportion and a definite feeling of deprivation and loss of prestige for many Vietnamese (Kelly, 1977; Liu and Muratta, 1977b).

Overall, the number one priority of the Task Force was to help the Vietnamese achieve economic self-sufficiency and thus ease their way into the mainstream of American life. Because of the recent economic recession in the United States and the typical refugee's lack of facility with the English language, low wages, underemployment, and underutilization of skills were common problems plaguing the refugees.

*Mental Depression.* Some preliminary data reveal that the economic and social pressures of American life are related to mental depression among the refugees. American physicians find this depression difficult to treat because modern psychiatric care is largely unknown to the Indochinese (Slote, 1972; 1977). Cultural and language barriers also prove hard to surmount. As Dale S. Haan, a staff director of the Senate Subcommittee on Refugees, recently observed, "There's a general depression . . . even among those who are employed" (Kneeland, 1977:16).

*Elderly Vietnamese.* Although few in number, those elderly Vietnamese who fled to the United States appear to face a combination of problems. Handicapped with no marketable skills or knowledge of English, the aged must cope as must other Vietnamese who lack these advantages. But the elderly must also cope with an alien cultural system which treats the aged as second class citizens, an experience they would not have encountered in their native country. In Vietnam the elderly are considered important, integral members of the family. While given deferential treatment, nevertheless they are expected to contribute in an active way to the needs of their society. This is in sharp contrast to the treatment afforded the elderly in America, where they are expected to behave in a helpless, even childlike manner (Yee and Van Arsdale, 1978).

The problems faced by the Vietnamese could have been minimized if the refugees had had a more realistic perception of their sponsors and if the sponsors had been given a better idea of the problems involved in the task they assumed. Sponsors often did not understand the refugees' expectations. Questions of employment availability often were pursued only superficially, and language problems were greatly underestimated (Justus, 1976).

31

Yet in spite of the hardships they endured and the many problems they faced, a study at Camp Pendleton reports that all refugees, regardless of age, expect to enjoy a higher life status in the future than they have ever known before (Liu and Muratta, 1978b). Has life in the United States measured up to these high expectations? Our next chapter looks at the results of five cross-sectional and longitudinal sample surveys conducted at five points in time since the refugees left the camps in late 1975. The results of these surveys should provide some information on the socio-economic status achieved by the Vietnamese refugees and their adjustment to life in a new land.

NOTES

1. The methods employed by both the U.S. Department of Health, Education, and Welfare (HEW) and the Immigration and Naturalization Service (INS) to collect data on the refugees fail to distinguish the country of origin of the respondent. In contrast, our data collected by Opportunity Systems, Inc., include only Vietnamese respondents. The latest figures based upon 170,698 refugees indicate that the vast majority (88 percent) are Vietnamese, and only 7 percent are Laotians and 5 percent Cambodians. Thus when we speak of the parameters of the entire population as reported by INS and HEW, it is not possible to make exact comparisons with our sample, as reported in Chapter 4, which is composed entirely of Vietnamese.

# Chapter 4

# Adapting To American Society:
# The Results of Five Sample Surveys

Between July 1975 and August 1977 five waves of telephone interview surveys were conducted to assess the socioeconomic adjustment of Vietnamese refugees to American society.[1] Conducted under the auspices of HEW, these rich and historically valuable sets of data provide documentation of one of the most massive evacuation and relocation efforts in history.[2] Of central interest are the data which report on the Vietnamese refugees' problems of adaptation and also indicate those areas in which the refugees have been most successful, socially and economically.

How large were the samples and how were they selected? We move now to a description of the methodology employed in the five surveys in order to answer these questions.

## FIRST WAVE SURVEY

During the last two weeks of August and the first week of September 1975, a first wave telephone survey was conducted to assess the status of Vietnamese refugees who had left the camps to be resettled in American communities as of July 15, 1975. This first wave sample is the first cross-sectional survey of the socio-economic status of Vietnamese refugees. These data serve as a benchmark for the four subsequent waves of survey data reported below.

The overall objective of the first wave survey was to determine major problems confronting the refugees in their new environment. It covered the refugees' background, employment, income, receipt of public assistance, education, and overall integration into American society. The data were collected by telephone interviews with a random sample of heads of households who had been resettled in communities across the country.[3]

*First Wave Sampling.* Of approximately 45,000 refugees released by mid-July 1975, adequate information on only 34,488 was available for sampling purposes. The Evacuee Master File included a complete enumeration of all refugees processed out of all resettlement camps in the United States. The sample was obtained by drawing every seventh individual from the Task Force's Evacuee Master File listings, with a random start at the seventh person. The total number of subjects thus selected was 4,926.

The principal difficulty with this sampling plan was the likelihood of oversampling large families. The probability of selecting a family of a given size "j" was j/7. To weight the sample properly on the basis of a given characteristic, e.g., the percent employed, a weight of 7/1 was given to families of size one, 7/2 to families of size two, 7/3 to families of size three, and so on. However, for any family of size seven or greater, a weight of 7/7 (1) was used.

Tables in the present paper report the weighted percentages obtained by using these weighting procedures. Each table reporting weighted percentages also gives the unweighted number of cases (N) for the group upon which each percentage is based.

The Evacuee Master File did not contain telephone numbers of the refugee or his or her sponsor, so it was necessary to conduct a search for the telephone numbers. Asking telephone directory assistance, using the sponsor's name and address, turned out to be of little value. Subsequently, 4,926 letters were mailed out under the auspices of HEW to each sampled respondent, notifying him or her of the forthcoming telephone survey and asking the respondent to provide his or her current telephone number and address. A total of 1,611 usable responses was received. The remainder was not usable for a variety of reasons: Some were not received by the cut-off date; some were returned, address unknown; and some failed to supply telephone numbers or gave incorrect numbers. Of the 1,611 usable responses, interviews were completed with 1,570 heads of households.[4]

SECOND WAVE SURVEY

In the latter part of November and early December 1975, a second wave telephone survey, similar in content to the first survey, was conducted to assess the status of refugees resettled as of October 15. The survey also followed up on some families who were interviewed in the first wave survey. The survey was designed to obtain further information on the refugees' background, employment, income, receipt of public assistance, education, and overall experience in adapting to American society.

*Second Wave Sampling.* Telephone interviews, with a national probability sample of heads of households were used in the second survey. The sample was designed to be representative of all refugees who had left the camps on or before October 15, 1975. The sample had two components. The first was a sample of 446 persons randomly drawn from the 1,570 heads of households who had responded to the first survey of refugees. The second component was a simple random sample of heads of households who had left the resettlement camps between July 16 and October 15. The sample of 2,930 heads of households resulted in 978 completed interviews.[5] Thus, combining 978 second wave respondents with 446 respondents from survey one, a total of 1,424 interviews was conducted with heads of households in survey two. These interviews with heads of households represented families totalling 7,498 individual members of whom 54.8 percent were males and 45.2 percent were females.

THIRD WAVE SURVEY

During the month of July and early August 1976, a third wave telephone survey was conducted. Telephone interviews were completed with 617 heads of households drawn from a population of all Vietnamese refugees resettled in the United States. These heads of households represent a total of 2,936 family members (hereafter referred to as the cross-sectional sample). A second

35

component of the third wave survey consisted of interviews with 398 heads of households representing 2,071 individual family members, who had been interviewed previously in both the first and second wave surveys (hereafter referred to as the longitudinal sample).

## FOURTH WAVE SURVEY

During March and April 1977, a fourth wave telephone survey was conducted. The sample consisted of all households with whom interviews were completed for the first time in survey three (N = 617) and a subsample of households who did not respond in survey three (N = 166), for a total initial sample of 783.

Telephone interviews were completed with 541 respondents from survey three and 104 nonrespondents from survey three, for a total actual sample of 645 heads of households. Thus, in survey four the overall response rate was 82 percent. This sample represents a cross-section of all Vietnamese refugees resettled in the United States and comprises a total of 2,949 individual family members. In projecting estimates for the entire Vietnamese refugee population as of the survey date, each of these 645 cases was weighted to reflect the demographic characteristics of all Vietnamese refugees resettled in the United States.

## FIFTH WAVE SURVEY

During the months of July and August 1977, a fifth wave telephone survey was conducted to assess further the status of the resettled Vietnamese refugees. The initial sample consisted of all heads of households with whom interviews were completed in survey four (N = 645). Telephone interviews were completed with 607 heads of households comprising a total of 2,817 persons, for an overall response rate of 94 percent. In projecting estimates for the entire Vietnamese refugee population as of the survey date, each of these 607 cases was weighted as in survey four.

## SAMPLE LIMITATIONS

It is critical to note that every sample survey has limitations. The present five surveys have the general strength of being both a national sample of Vietnamese refugees as well as a random probability sample. In addition, the data were collected by 40 Vietnamese interviewers.[6] The outright respondent refusal rate is less than one-half of 1 percent. The remainder of the nonrespondents represents individuals who could not be located after their release from the resettlement camps. A study of nonrespondents from survey one was conducted. When these nonrespondents were compared to the respondents in survey one, no statistically significant differences were revealed.

In general, when we look at age, sex, education, and date of release from camp, the actual sample appears to approximate the entire population quite closely. (See Appendix B.) We turn now to an examination of the data collected from the five sample surveys.[7]

## PROFILE OF VIETNAMESE REFUGEE SAMPLE[8]

Upon arriving in the United States, the Vietnamese refugees were dispersed among four refugee camps. With 42.8 percent of the refugee population, Fort Chaffee had the plurality of refugees represented in the sample. It was followed by California's Camp Pendleton which had more than one out of every three respondents (35.7 percent). Eglin Air Force Base in Florida and Pennsylvania's Fort Indiantown Gap each had approximately 11 percent.

The results of the first wave survey reveal that after the relocation of refugees was effected, the Southern and Western regions of the United States each had approximately one-third of the refugees. The North Central region had nearly 20 percent of the refugees and the North Eastern region had approximately 10 percent.[9]

The United States' refugee policy specified that there were only four ways in which the refugees could be released from camps: (1) they could be repatriated; (2) they could be relocated to another country; (3) they could prove financial solvency (each family member must have $4,000); or, (4) they could have sponsors in the United States who would be willing to assume both personal and financial responsibility (Hohl, 1978; Kelly, 1977; U.S., Congress, Senate, 1978). Most refugees in our sample left the camps via the sponsorship method. Only 1 percent left camp by one of the other three ways. A majority (56 percent) of the sponsors were families. Approximately 25 percent of the sponsors were groups and 16 percent were individuals.

37

Group sponsorships were usually arranged with the help of the National Voluntary Resettlement Agencies (VOLAGs). The largest number of group sponsorships (35 percent) was undertaken by the United States Catholic Conference. The International Rescue Committee and the Lutheran Immigration and Refugee Service each had approximately 17 percent of the group sponsorships in our sample.[10]

A look at the residential distribution of the refugees indicates that they reside in all 50 states, the District of Columbia, Guam, and American Samoa. At first, the four states where the refugee camps were located took a disproportionate number of refugees as residents, but as we shall see later, this pattern may be changing.

*Age, Sex, and Education.* Our sample is decidedly young. Four out of ten respondents are under 15 years of age, and more than eight out of ten are younger than 35. At the other end of the age spectrum, fewer than 2 percent are over 65 years of age. Fifty-two percent of our sample are males and 48 percent females.

Forty percent of the Vietnamese have a secondary education and more than ten percent have a university education. Fifteen percent, however, have only a primary degree, and 20 percent have no formal education.

*Household Composition.* Slightly more than one-third (34 percent) of the refugee households in our sample consist of six or more persons, and approximately 5 percent consist of ten or more persons. Two factors might account for the relatively large size of refugee households. First, the Vietnamese typically have more children than the average American family, and second, the Vietnamese traditionally live within an extended family context.

We can speculate about the importance of the extended family upon the refugees' socioeconomic and psychological adaptation. On the one hand, from an economic point of view, there are more mouths to feed in a large family. On the other hand, there are potentially more family members to contribute to the overall household income. In addition, an extended family is supportive, offering its members psychological comfort and cultural reinforcement.

*Occupation in Vietnam.* A high proportion of our respondents report that in Vietnam they were employed as professionals, clerical and sales workers, and managers. Our findings (Table

4.1) indicate that two-thirds of the heads of households were white-collar workers while the remaining one-third were blue-collar. Looking first at the white-collar group, we note that a plurality (45 percent) were professionals. One-third were clerical and sales workers and one-fifth (22 percent) were managers in Vietnam. Of the refugees with blue-collar backgrounds, over four in ten (44.4 percent) were craftsmen, 10.5 percent were operatives and transport workers, and the remainder (45.1 percent) were distributed among a number of other blue-collar occupations.

What are the economic prospects for the Vietnamese refugees? Will the refugees from white-collar backgrounds with more education, training, and entrepreneurial expertise gain an economic foothold in American society more quickly than their blue-collar counterparts who were trained as craftsmen and operatives?

## CHANGING SOCIOECONOMIC STATUS

*Occupational Status.* Results from the fifth wave survey (Table 4.1) reveal that there has been a considerable amount of downward mobility for Vietnamese heads of households. Of the 319 Vietnamese who held white-collar jobs in Vietnam, more than six in ten (60.6 percent) now hold blue-collar jobs. The remainder hold white-collar jobs, with a plurality occupying clerical and sales positions. The data indicate that there has been considerable downward mobility among the professionals. Of the 142 Vietnamese refugees who were employed as professionals in Vietnam, fewer than one in five (17.7 percent) has been able to find similar work in the United States. One in four has taken a clerical, sales, or managerial job. Of those professionals who moved into blue-collar work, a plurality have taken work as craftsmen.

Those Vietnamese who were managers in Vietnam have had even more difficulty than professionals in transferring their managerial status to their newly adopted country. A mere one in twenty (5.1 percent) has been successful. Like the professionals, a plurality (30.5 percent) have become craftsmen. Approximately one in four has taken employment in other blue-collar fields and one in five has found employment in the clerical and sales fields.

Clerical and sales personnel have experienced the least downward mobility among the three white-collar categories. More than one in three respondents has been able to assume a similar position in the United States. Interestingly, approximately 6 percent of those refugees from clerical and sales backgrounds report they have experienced upward mobility, moving into the professional or managerial ranks. Clearly, sales and clerical jobs seem to be the most accessible to the Vietnamese in the United States.

When we look at the mobility patterns of blue-collar employees (Table 4.1), we see less downward mobility among blue-collar Vietnamese than among their white-collar counterparts. Over four in ten (44.2 percent) of the craftsmen, for example, have been able to translate their Vietnam-acquired technical skills to their newly adopted country. Interestingly, almost four in ten of those employed as operatives and in transport have taken work as craftsmen in the United States. A plurality (43.7 percent), however, have moved into other blue-collar pursuits. Often this move represents a downward occupational shift.

Of those respondents in other blue-collar jobs (Table 4.1), we find that a plurality, exactly 33.3 percent, of the Vietnamese have moved into the same field, while over one-quarter (28.5 percent) have gained employment as craftsmen.

We note that a majority of the heads of households had white-collar origins, and, generally, the white-collar Vietnamese have suffered the highest rates of downward mobility. Blue-collar workers have been more successful in translating their Vietnamese training into similar occupational niches in the United States.

Of the white-collar workers, the Vietnamese in clerical and sales positions have translated their skills most easily to their new milieu. The general inability of white-collar Vietnamese to transfer their occupational status in Vietnam to the United States may be attributed to two central factors. First, there is a greater need for language fluency and interpersonal skills in the white-collar sector of the economy. Managers, in particular, would be hardest hit in attempting to translate their supervisory skills to the United States. Superior interpersonal skills are a prerequisite for gaining entry into the managerial ranks. Secondly, there is a relatively long time lag before physicians and dentists can obtain the required U.S. licenses, even with the assistance of VOLAG-sponsored programs to speed this process. These programs provided a $250-per-month stipend for the retraining of physicians and dentists to meet U.S. requirements (U.S. Department of Health, Education, and Welfare, 1976a).[11]

## TABLE 4.1

### PRESENT OCCUPATION OF HEADS OF HOUSEHOLDS BY VIETNAM OCCUPATION (WEIGHTED PERCENTAGES)

| Vietnam Occupation | Total | | White-Collar | | | Present Occupation Blue-Collar | | | |
|---|---|---|---|---|---|---|---|---|---|
| | N | % | Professional | Manager | Clerical and Sales | Craftsmen | Operatives & Transport | Laborers | Other Blue-Collar |
| *Total* | 472 | 100.2 | 7.0 | 2.3 | 18.7 | 29.5 | 11.5 | 7.2 | 24.0 |
| *White-Collar* | 319 | 100.0 | 10.3 | 3.5 | 25.6 | 26.1 | 9.0 | 4.0 | 21.5 |
| Professional | 142 | 99.9 | 17.7 | 3.9 | 20.1 | 29.1 | 10.5 | 1.7 | 16.9 |
| Managers | 71 | 100.0 | 4.0 | 5.1 | 22.5 | 30.5 | 11.8 | 2.7 | 23.4 |
| Clerical & Sales | 106 | 100.0 | 4.3 | 2.1 | 34.1 | 19.9 | 5.6 | 7.7 | 26.3 |
| *Blue-Collar* | 153 | 100.0 | .9 | — | 5.8 | 35.7 | 16.0 | 13.1 | 28.5 |
| Craftsmen | 68 | 100.1 | 2.3 | — | 6.0 | 44.2 | 16.7 | 12.4 | 18.5 |
| Operatives & Transport | 16 | 100.0 | — | — | — | 38.2 | 4.8 | 13.3 | 43.7 |
| Laborers | — | | — | — | — | — | — | — | — |
| Other Blue-Collar | 69 | 99.9 | — | — | 6.8 | 28.5 | 17.8 | 13.5 | 33.3 |

*General Employment Characteristics.* Since arriving in the United States, most of the Vietnamese have found jobs. The men have been somewhat more successful than the women. Over two-thirds (68.2 percent) of the men were employed when interviewed in the first survey in July and August 1975 (Table 4.2). By January 1976, the time of the second survey, this rate had increased to over eight in ten (82.0 percent). In the third survey, September 1976, the rate was nearly nine in ten, and by the time of the fifth survey, September and October 1977, the rate had risen to a remarkable 95 percent.

Similarly, the overall rates of employment for women 16 years of age and older increased during the same time frame (Table 4.3). At first a bare majority (50.9 percent) were employed. In survey two the employment rate had increased to seven in ten (70.1 percent). By the third survey the rate was eight in ten (82.0 percent), which increased to 86.4 percent in the fourth survey, and a remarkable 93.2 percent in the fifth survey.

These findings are particularly noteworthy since they are averages for all men and women 16 years of age and over. A breakdown of the respondents by their relationships to the heads of households is presented in Table 4.2. The relationships include spouses, children, grandchildren, nephews, nieces, more distant relatives, and persons unrelated to the head of the household. The results of the first survey reveal some variation in the employment rates for men according to their relationships to heads of households. Employment rates for the men range from a low of 50 percent for those respondents who are unrelated to the head of household to a high of 70.6 percent for those who were grandchildren and nephews. In contrast, the fifth survey reveals essentially no variation in the level of employment by relationship to heads of households.

Except for one category, the employment rates for women in the first survey showed little variation among relationships to the head of household. (See Table 4.3.) Only one in four (27.9 percent) of the women who were parents or spouses was employed. In the other categories about half the women were working. By the fifth survey the percentage had changed radically. Three categories (grandchildren and nieces, parents and spouses, and other relatives) had reached 100 percent employment, and the average employment rate of women in all relationships was 93.2 percent.

## TABLE 4.2

### EMPLOYMENT STATUS OF PERSONS 16 YEARS AND OLDER BY SEX AND RELATIONSHIP TO HEADS OF HOUSEHOLD IN SURVEYS I, II, III, IV, AND V
#### (WEIGHTED PERCENTAGES)

Males

| Relationship to Head of Household | Survey I | | Survey II | | Survey III | | Survey IV | | Survey V | |
|---|---|---|---|---|---|---|---|---|---|---|
| | Un-weighted N | % Employed | Un-weighted N | % Employed | Un-weighted N | % Employed | Un-weighted N | % Employed | Un-weighted N | % Employed |
| *Total* | 1887 | 68.2 | 1988 | 82.0 | 764 | 89.9 | 704 | 94.6 | 705 | 95.1 |
| Head | 1110 | 68.1 | 1119 | 82.9 | 489 | 90.6 | 497 | 93.8 | 473 | 94.4 |
| Spouse | 38 | 63.0 | 16 | 68.7 | 5 | 100.0 | 8 | 100.0 | 12 | 100.0 |
| Child or spouse of child | 303 | 67.5 | 198 | 78.8 | 107 | 89.7 | 76 | 95.4 | 94 | 97.1 |
| Grandchild or nephew | 44 | 70.6 | 44 | 81.8 | 9 | 88.9 | 10 | 100.0 | 8 | 100.0 |
| Parent or spouse | 21 | 54.1 | 15 | 60.0 | 10 | 80.0 | 8 | 100.0 | 3 | 100.0 |
| Other relative | 356 | 69.1 | 284 | 77.1 | 72 | 83.3 | 56 | 96.9 | 60 | 92.7 |
| Unrelated | 15 | 50.0 | 312 | 87.2 | 72 | 93.1 | 49 | 96.9 | 55 | 98.6 |

43

## Table 4.3

### Employment Status of Persons 16 Years and Older By Sex and Relationship to Heads of Household in Surveys I, II, III, IV, and V
### (Weighted Percentages)

### Females

| Relationship to Head of Household | Survey I | | Survey II | | Survey III | | Survey IV | | Survey V | |
|---|---|---|---|---|---|---|---|---|---|---|
| | Unweighted N | % Employed | Unweighted N | % Employed | Unweighted N | % Employed | Unweighted N | % Employed | Unweighted N | % Employed |
| *Total* | 1122 | 50.9 | 789 | 70.1 | 327 | 82.0 | 318 | 86.4 | 354 | 93.2 |
| Head | 194 | 53.7 | 121 | 80.2 | 47 | 91.5 | 50 | 85.4 | 53 | 92.5 |
| Spouse | 352 | 46.2 | 264 | 64.8 | 131 | 77.9 | 160 | 84.8 | 176 | 91.7 |
| Child or spouse of child | 276 | 52.9 | 190 | 72.1 | 73 | 86.3 | 52 | 92.0 | 75 | 92.6 |
| Grandchild or niece | 28 | 51.5 | 10 | 70.0 | 9 | 66.7 | 4 | 100.0 | 4 | 100.0 |
| Parent or spouse | 16 | 27.9 | 11 | 72.8 | 7 | 42.9 | 5 | 68.0 | 2 | 100.0 |
| Other relative | 244 | 55.1 | 174 | 68.4 | 59 | 84.7 | 45 | 89.8 | 44 | 100.0 |
| Unrelated | 12 | 53.1 | 19 | 73.7 | 1 | 100.0 | 2 | 50.0 | — | — |

*Employment by Age and Sex.* Table 4.4 shows the relationship between a respondent's age, sex, and employment. In the first survey both the youngest (16-24 years) and oldest (45 years and over) males had the lowest level of employment (52.1 percent and 64.2 percent, respectively). The rates of employment for men of all ages increased over the four subsequent surveys. Thus, by the fifth survey there is essentially no difference by age for male employment. The average percentage of men employed, regardless of age, is 95.1 percent.

The employment rates of the women follow a similar trend, with one general exception: Employment rates for those age 45 and over are substantially less than the rates for other age categories. (See Table 4.5.) Whereas nine out of ten of those under 45 are employed, only seven out of ten of those women 45 and over are employed.

*Employment by Proficiency in English.* Respondents were asked if they could understand, speak, read, or write English. The data in Table 4.6 compare employment rates by the refugees' proficiency in English as reported in four surveys, Wave I, Wave II, Wave III, and Wave V. These data were not collected in the fourth survey.

Interestingly, proficiency is related largely to rates of employment only in the first survey. Even then, a majority of those Vietnamese who report no English language proficiency still have managed to land a job. For those respondents who report they have a good command of English, the rate of employment increases to approximately two-thirds.

The overall employment rates increased after the first survey from 62.7 percent in the first, to nearly 80 percent in the second, almost 90 percent in the third, and reach 94.5 percent in the fifth. Remarkably, the fifth survey reports that regardless of English language proficiency, approximately nine in ten of the Vietnamese refugees are employed (Table 4.6). The rate of employment for those reporting that they do not understand English at all is 88.8 percent; for those who speak, read, and write English well, the employment rate increases to 97 percent. It is difficult to explain the virtual lack of a relationship between English language proficiency and the rate of employment. One interpretation suggests that the personal sponsors and the VOLAGs generally have been very effective in finding employment for the refugees. In most in-

## Table 4.4

### Employment Status of Persons 16 Years and Older By Age and Sex in Surveys I, II, III, IV, and V

#### (Weighted Percentages)

#### Males

| Age | Survey I | | Survey II | | Survey III | | Survey IV | | Survey V | |
|---|---|---|---|---|---|---|---|---|---|---|
| | Un-weighted N | % Employed | Un-weighted N | % Employed | Un-weighted N | % Employed | Un-weighted N | % Employed | Un-weighted N | % Employed |
| *Total* | 1888 | 68.2 | 1988 | 82.0 | 764 | 89.9 | 704 | 94.6 | 705 | 95.1 |
| 16 - 24 | 550 | 64.2 | 743 | 82.4 | 234 | 88.0 | 197 | 97.1 | 217 | 95.2 |
| 25 - 34 | 578 | 75.6 | 687 | 82.7 | 270 | 91.9 | 246 | 95.3 | 238 | 95.7 |
| 35 - 44 | 451 | 71.1 | 347 | 82.7 | 152 | 92.8 | 146 | 93.5 | 140 | 97.5 |
| 45 & over | 309 | 52.1 | 211 | 77.7 | 108 | 85.2 | 115 | 90.1 | 110 | 90.6 |

## Table 4.5
### Employment Status of Persons 16 Years and Older By Age and Sex in Surveys I, II, III, IV, and V
#### (Weighted Percentages)

F e m a l e s

| Age | Survey I | | Survey II | | Survey III | | Survey IV | | Survey V | |
|---|---|---|---|---|---|---|---|---|---|---|
| | Un-weighted N | % Employed | Un-weighted N | % Employed | Un-weighted N | % Employed | Un-weighted N | % Employed | Un-weighted N | % Employed |
| *Total* | 1120 | 50.9 | 789 | 70.1 | 327 | 82.0 | 318 | 86.4 | 354 | 93.2 |
| 16 - 24 | 446 | 51.5 | 310 | 72.6 | 109 | 84.4 | 86 | 88.2 | 113 | 93.1 |
| 25 - 34 | 406 | 51.0 | 295 | 70.8 | 121 | 82.6 | 126 | 87.9 | 129 | 95.6 |
| 35 - 44 | 205 | 53.2 | 123 | 65.8 | 67 | 83.6 | 73 | 84.0 | 81 | 96.7 |
| 45 & over | 63 | 41.3 | 61 | 62.3 | 30 | 66.6 | 33 | 80.3 | 31 | 73.3 |

## Table 4.6

### Employment Status of Persons 16 Years and Older By Proficiency in English in Surveys I, II, III, and V*
### (Weighted Percentages)

| Proficiency in English | Survey I Unweighted N | Survey I % Employed | Survey II Unweighted N | Survey II % Employed | Survey III Unweighted N | Survey III % Employed | Survey V Unweighted N | Survey V % Employed |
|---|---|---|---|---|---|---|---|---|
| *Total* | 2988** | 62.7 | 2003 | 78.4 | 1091 | 87.5 | 1059 | 94.5 |
| *Understand English* | | | | | | | | |
| Not at all | 127 | 56.7 | 155 | 71.0 | 47 | 72.3 | 25 | 88.8 |
| Some | 1856 | 60.6 | 1481 | 78.5 | 794 | 87.5 | 672 | 93.4 |
| Well | 975 | 67.8 | 363 | 81.0 | 250 | 90.4 | 362 | 97.1 |
| *Speak English* | | | | | | | | |
| Not at all | 141 | 53.2 | 161 | 70.8 | 50 | 72.0 | 27 | 90.1 |
| Some | 1873 | 60.9 | 1484 | 78.6 | 790 | 87.0 | 681 | 93.5 |
| Well | 946 | 68.1 | 355 | 80.8 | 251 | 90.4 | 351 | 97.0 |
| *Read English* | | | | | | | | |
| Not at all | 142 | 52.8 | 173 | 69.9 | 59 | 72.9 | 38 | 92.3 |
| Some | 1791 | 61.4 | 1432 | 78.8 | 768 | 87.5 | 689 | 93.4 |
| Well | 1024 | 66.7 | 393 | 80.4 | 264 | 90.9 | 332 | 97.3 |
| *Write English* | | | | | | | | |
| Not at all | 155 | 53.5 | 179 | 70.4 | 59 | 74.6 | 38 | 92.6 |
| Some | 1812 | 61.5 | 1444 | 78.7 | 769 | 87.4 | 704 | 93.5 |
| Well | 991 | 66.7 | 376 | 80.6 | 263 | 90.9 | 317 | 97.1 |

* Data not available in survey four.

** Due to a small percentage of nonrespondents, the N columns for surveys one and two do not necessarily total 2988 and 2003 respectively.

stances, however, the refugees have accepted employment far below the status of their former jobs in Vietnam.

*Job-hunting Methods.* Of those Vietnamese who remained unemployed by the time the fifth survey (August 1977) went into the field, most report that they are using conventional means of finding employment. Two-thirds (66.5 percent) of the job seekers directly contact employers; six in ten (61.4 percent) use the services of employment agencies. Over one-quarter (26.9 percent) are aided by friends and relatives, and a similar number answer classified advertisements. Interestingly, fewer than 3 percent are aided by their sponsors at this stage of resettlement.[12]

*Reasons for Not Seeking Employment.* Of those respondents who report they are not employed, a plurality said they are currently enrolled in school. This figure has tended to increase in each survey from approximately one-third (35.5 percent) of the respondents in the first survey to nearly a majority (48.2 percent) in the most recent survey. Another reason for not seeking employment is "keeping house," which nearly one-third (29.8 percent) report. One in five (21.3 percent) reports poor health as the primary reason. Consistent with earlier findings, the percentage of respondents reporting lack of English language proficiency as the reason for not seeking employment has declined for the most part across the five surveys. In the first survey it was nearly one in five and in the fifth survey it is fewer than one in ten persons (Table 4.7).

*Hours, Personal Income, and Household Income.* Table 4.8 reports that the proportion of refugees working full time (40 or more hours per week) has increased in each of the four surveys.[13] Three-quarters of the refugees were working 40 or more hours in the second survey and over eight in ten are working full time in the fifth survey.

In general, the findings indicate that the refugees' total weekly income increased between surveys two and five.[14] The percentage of respondents earning $100 to $199 per week moved from four in ten (44.4 percent) in the second survey to more than six in ten (63.3 percent) by the fifth survey. The number of those at the highest rungs of the income ladder, persons earning $200 or more per week, increased from a mere 3 percent to more than 14 percent in the fifth survey (Table 4.9).

## TABLE 4.7

### REASONS FOR NOT SEEKING EMPLOYMENT
### IN SURVEYS I, II, III, IV, AND V*
### (WEIGHTED PERCENTAGES)

| Reasons | Survey I | Survey II | Survey III | Survey IV | Survey V |
|---|---|---|---|---|---|
| *Total* | *259* | *1723* | *612* | *663* | *545* |
| Attending school | 35.5 | 34.4 | 49.2 | 56.0 | 48.2 |
| Keeping house | 17.3 | 32.2 | 36.6 | 28.2 | 29.8 |
| Poor health | 6.5 | 14.1 | 13.2 | 17.7 | 21.3 |
| Poor English | 19.3 | 19.0 | 11.3 | 14.9 | 9.1 |
| Other means of support | 10.8 | 3.5 | 2.5 | 1.6 | .5 |
| Discouraged | — | 1.1 | .3 | .1 | .4 |
| Other | 17.0 | 5.5 | 3.1 | 2.1 | 3.1 |

* NOTE: Columns do not necessarily total 100 percent since respondents were able to report more than one category.

## TABLE 4.8

### HOURS WORKED PER WEEK FOR EMPLOYED PERSONS
### IN SURVEYS II, III, IV, AND V*
### (WEIGHTED PERCENTAGES)

| Hours Worked | Survey II | Survey III | Survey IV | Survey V |
|---|---|---|---|---|
| *Total* | *2184* | *955* | *940* | *998* |
| Less than 15 | 4.1 | 2.5 | 1.9 | 1.3 |
| 15 - 29 | 9.8 | 10.5 | 10.1 | 10.3 |
| 30 - 39 | 9.5 | 7.3 | 7.7 | 4.3 |
| 40+ | 76.0 | 79.7 | 80.0 | 84.1 |
| N/A | .5 | — | .2 | — |

* These data were not collected for survey one.

In the first survey on household income, a plurality (42.1 percent) of the Vietnamese households earned less than $200 per month (Table 4.10). The results of the fifth survey indicate that this has declined to a mere 3 percent. In contrast, the percentage of households earning $800 or more per month increased from approximately one in seven (14.9 percent) to more than half of the households (51.4 percent). Thus the typical annual income of refugee households is more than $9,600 in 1977. This compares to a median household income of $13,572 for the United States as a whole.[15]

TABLE 4.9

WEEKLY WAGES AND SALARY INCOME
IN SURVEYS II, III, IV, AND V*
(WEIGHTED PERCENTAGES)

| Weekly Wages and Income Level | Survey II | Survey III | Survey IV | Survey V |
|---|---|---|---|---|
| *Total* | *2184* | *955* | *940* | *998* |
| None | 1.9 | — | — | 1.3 |
| Under $50 | 10.5 | 8.0 | 6.4 | 4.9 |
| $50 - 99 | 40.0 | 27.6 | 16.9 | 16.2 |
| $100 - 199 | 44.4 | 57.6 | 65.2 | 63.3 |
| $200 - over | 3.2 | 5.3 | 9.9 | 14.3 |
| N/A | — | 1.5 | 1.6 | — |

* NOTE: Income data were not collected for survey one.

TABLE 4.10

MONTHLY INCOME OF REFUGEE HOUSEHOLDS FROM ALL SOURCES
IN SURVEYS I, II, III, IV, AND V
(WEIGHTED PERCENTAGES)

|  | Survey I | Survey II | Survey III | Survey IV | Survey V |
|---|---|---|---|---|---|
| *Total* | *1570* | *1424* | *617* | *645* | *607* |
| Under $200 | 42.1 | 17.6 | 5.3 | 4.0 | 3.2 |
| $200 - 399 | 14.2 | 15.4 | 13.1 | 11.0 | 7.8 |
| $400 - 599 | 17.3 | 20.9 | 22.2 | 22.0 | 20.6 |
| $600 - 799 | 11.5 | 13.6 | 13.9 | 16.2 | 14.0 |
| $800 - over | 14.9 | 32.4 | 41.2 | 43.8 | 51.4 |
| N/A | — | — | 4.2 | 2.8 | 3.1 |

Perhaps even more salient, over ninety percent of household income is in the form of wages and salaries. That is, for every $100 of household income, 90.8 percent comes from wages and salaries. Federal assistance accounts for the remaining proportion of household income (Table 4.11).

*Public Assistance.* The percentage of households receiving federal assistance increased from survey one to survey three, but decreased in the two most recent surveys. In the first survey (Table 4.12) approximately four in ten (39.6 percent) of the refugee households were receiving federal assistance in the form of food stamps, medical aid, and social security. Currently, fewer than one in three (32.0 percent) are receiving public assistance. These findings are consistent with the increasing rate of employment and overall progress toward self-sufficiency. Thus one can speculate that the decline in the percentage receiving assistance is likely to continue.

## TABLE 4.11

MONTHLY HOUSEHOLD INCOME FROM ALL SOURCES BY
COMPONENTS OF INCOME IN TERMS OF PERCENT OF DOLLAR
CONTRIBUTIONS TO HOUSEHOLD INCOME IN SURVEYS III, IV AND V*
(WEIGHTED PERCENTAGES)

|  | Survey III | Survey IV | Survey V |
|---|---|---|---|
| Total Households | 617 | 645 | 607 |
| Wages and Salary | 90.4 | 87.9 | 90.8 |
| Refugee Financial Assistance | 6.7 | 8.2 | 6.1 |
| SSI** | 1.2 | 1.4 | 1.5 |
| Other | 1.7 | 2.5 | 1.6 |

* NOTE: These data were not collected in surveys one and two.
** Supplementary Security Income.

## TABLE 4.12

TYPES OF FEDERAL ASSISTANCE RECEIVED BY REFUGEE HOUSEHOLDS
IN SURVEYS I, II, III, IV, AND V*
(WEIGHTED PERCENTAGES)

| Types of Assistance | Survey I | Survey II | Survey III | Survey IV | Survey V |
|---|---|---|---|---|---|
| Total | 1568 | 1424 | 617 | 645 | 607 |
| Percent Receiving Assistance | 39.6 | 42.0 | 49.9 | 33.4** | 32.0** |
| Food Stamps | 21.4 | 25.6 | 24.7 | 24.7 | 22.8 |
| Medical Assistance | 17.9 | 23.7 | 42.8 | N/A | N/A |
| Refugee Financial Assistance | 18.2 | 13.4 | 19.8 | 23.4 | 20.9 |
| SSI | .5 | 2.8 | 6.3 | 6.5 | 7.4 |
| Other | 1.6 | — | — | — | — |

* NOTE: Columns do not necessarily total 100 percent since respondents were able to report more than one category.

** NOTE: Does not include medical assistance. Information from States indicates 47.6 percent of refugees were eligible for medical assistance as of March 1, 1977, and 46.1 percent as of August 1, 1977. Household data are not available.

SUMMARY

In general, data from five waves of telephone interview surveys reveal that the Vietnamese are making substantial progress as they adjust socioeconomically to life in the United States. All but 1 percent of the refugees in the sample left the resettlement camps via sponsorship, with more than half sponsored by families. The sample consists of a young, relatively well-educated group of refugees. Many of the respondents had fled Vietnam in large family groups. More than one in three of the households represented consists of six or more persons. The sample is predominately a white-collar group. Two out of three heads of households are white-collar workers and the remaining one-third are blue-collar.

The findings reveal considerable downward occupational mobility, particularly among refugees who formerly held professional and managerial positions. The high degree of English language fluency and interpersonal skills required in these occupations probably accounts for the difficulties encountered by professionals and managers. In fact, a plurality in these two categories are working as craftsmen at the time of survey five. Clerical and sales personnel have demonstrated the least downward mobility among white-collar workers. Blue-collar workers, however, have been the most successful of all in translating their skills to American jobs.

Employment rates among the Vietnamese are remarkably high. Ninety-five percent of males and 93.2 percent of females have found jobs. The employment rates for men increase steadily with age. The women follow a similar trend except for those age 45 and over, for whom employment rates decline.

Proficiency in English is related to employment rates only in survey one. After that time there appears to be no relationship between the two. In fact, a large majority of those who report no English language proficiency nevertheless have jobs.

By the time of survey five over 80 percent are working full time as opposed to part time. Income among the refugees has increased steadily over time. By 1977, the typical annual household income of Vietnamese refugees was $9,600. Most notably, over 90 percent of this income consists of wages and salaries. Fewer than one-third of the Vietnamese households are presently receiving

54

public assistance of any type, a clear indication that the Vietnamese are moving steadily toward economic self-sufficiency.

Where does this socioeconomic progress lead, as the Vietnamese adjust more fully to life in America? Will they become assimilated into the mainstream of American society? In Chapter Five we propose a sociohistorical model which attemps to predict the future of the Vietnamese in America.

## NOTES

1. We use the term "wave" (i.e., First Wave Survey, Second Wave Survey, etc.) to be consistent with the terminology used by the contract research firm, Opportunity Systems, Inc., which collected the survey data. Thus the term "wave" suggests an anticipation of succeeding and repeated surveys that are forthcoming.

2. See Opportunity Systems, Inc. (1975; 1976a; 1976b; 1977a; 1977b).

3. Heads of households were determined by self-definition. In order to obtain a representative sample, only one person was interviewed from any single household. When the head of household was unavailable for interview, another responsible adult in that family was selected to respond in his place, supplying demographic information on that person.

4. Although the contract research firm which collected the data for HEW did not always report the number of refugees in the entire population from which they drew their sample or the overall response rate, they did provide the total number of respondents who were interviewed. However, they did not always provide complete information regarding the number of nonrespondents. Thus we are unable to compute a precise overall response rate. Nguyen Minh Chau, Project Director for Opportunity Systems, Inc., indicates, however, that they met HEW's requirement of a minimum of 60 to 65 percent overall response rate. Additionally, the outright respondent refusal rate for all five surveys was less than one-half of 1 percent. In sum, it is useful to note that, given the unique nature of the sample and the strict deadlines which had to be met, these overall response rates compare favorably to those reported in standard telephone interview surveys (Dillman, 1978; Montero, 1976).

5. See note 4.

6. Source: personal communication with Nguyen Minh Chau, Project Director, Opportunity Systems, Inc., January 9, 1979.

7. Since we did not have access to the study's original data tapes, we were not able to generate new statistical tables for analysis. Rather, our study is necessarily limited to the data made available to us by Opportunity Systems, Inc.

8. Our demographic profile is based upon data collected from survey one. The figures represent not only heads of households but also individual family members within those households.

9. Regions and their respective states were categorized as follows: North Eastern Region (Maine, Connecticut, New Hampshire, Vermont, Massachusetts, Rhode Island, New York, New Jersey, Pennsylvania); North Central Region (Ohio, Indiana, Illinois, Michigan, Wisconsin, Minnesota, Iowa, Missouri, North Dakota, South Dakota, Nebraska, Kansas); Southern Region (Delaware, Maryland, District of Columbia, Virginia, West Virginia, North Carolina, South Carolina, Georgia, Florida, Kentucky, Tennessee, Alabama, Mississippi, Arkansas, Louisiana, Oklahoma, Texas); Western Region (Montana, Idaho, Wyoming, Colorado, New Mexico, Arizona, Utah, Nevada, Washington, Oregon, California, Alaska, Hawaii); U.S. possessions (Guam, American Samoa).

10. Other major VOLAGs involved and the percentage of the refugees in our sample which they processed include: Church World Service (11.2 percent), United HIAS Service (3.9 percent), Tolstoy Foundation (2.4 percent), and American Fund for Czechoslovak Refugees (.6 percent).

11. It is important to note that these rates of mobility are available only for heads of households and not for the entire sample of Vietnamese.

12. Since respondents were asked to report all job-hunting methods they were using, the percentages total more than 100 percent.

13. The data regarding the proportion of refugees working full time were not collected for survey one.

14. Income data were not collected for survey one.

15. Source: personal communication, U.S. Bureau of the Census, January 25, 1979.

# Chapter 5

# Toward the Assimilation
# of the Vietnamese Immigrants

A Theory of Spontaneous International Migration (SIM)

In a study of general migration patterns, Kunz (1973) divides refugee movements into two classifications, anticipatory and acute. Anticipatory refugees are those who leave home in an orderly way after some preparation. The prospects are good, Kunz observes, for these refugees to adjust satisfactorily to life in a new land. Acute refugees, on the other hand, are those who flee in the wake of massive political and military upheaval. These refugees flee en masse or in bursts of groups with the emphasis on escape. Kunz suggests that the acute refugees might face more difficult problems of adjustment than the anticipatory group.

On the one hand, because the Vietnamese hastily left their homeland, they would appear to be acute refugees. On the other hand, their background is more typical of anticipatory refugees who tend to be relatively well-educated and somewhat familiar with the culture of the country to which they are going. Many of the refugees were familiar with American culture and language prior to their departure. Even before the Americans arrived in Vietnam, Western culture was know to many Vietnamese because of the French presence.

Thus, while Kunz's (1973) refugee classifications are helpful, they are somewhat inadequate as applied to the Vietnamese experience. Aspects of both the acute and anticipatory refugee patterns appear to merge, forming a unique refugee group. We shall call this third distinct pattern of refugee movement Spontaneous International Migration (SIM). In the Vietnam situation, the people were compelled to leave their native country abruptly due to circumstances which they perceived as life-threatening. Most arrived in the United States after little or no prior preparation and with no concrete plans for the future. Their previous working relationship with Americans in Vietnam, however, gave them some advantage as they faced life in a new land. This situation is in direct contrast to early Asian immigrants who, unlike the Vietnamese, came to America after a period of planning and with a definite goal in mind. The anticipatory socialization the refugees had experienced in Vietnam might facilitate their socioeconomic adaptation and assimilation in the United States. Thus, the unique phenomenon of Vietnamese flight and resettlement in the United States appears to call for new theoretical explanations.

SPONTANEOUS INTERNATIONAL MIGRATION (SIM): A MODEL OF VIETNAMESE IMMIGRATION AND RESETTLEMENT IN THE UNITED STATES

Figure 5.1 presents a schematic diagram of two different immigration patterns which we suggest bring about different migrant outcomes. Represented here are two different models of immigration: The early Asian (Chinese and Japanese) immigration experience (Ichihashi, 1932; Kitano, 1976; Levine and Montero, 1973; Lyman, 1974; Miyamoto, 1939; Montero, 1978a) and the Vietnamese pattern which we term Spontaneous International Migration (SIM). The discussion below presents the sociohistorical processes which unfold in three phases as illustrated in Figure 5.1.

58

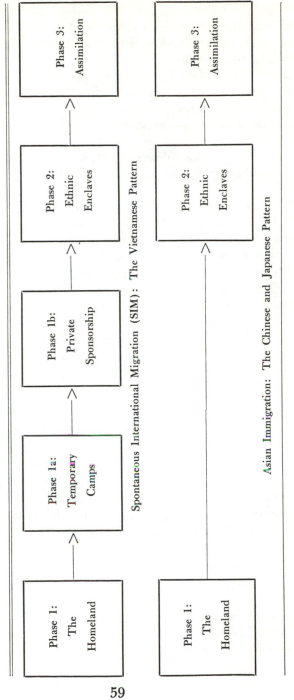

FIGURE 5.1

SPONTANEOUS INTERNATIONAL MIGRATION (SIM):
A MODEL OF VIETNAMESE IMMIGRATION AND RESETTLEMENT IN THE UNITED STATES

| Phase 1:<br>The<br>Homeland | > | Phase 1a:<br>Temporary<br>Camps | > | Phase 1b:<br>Private<br>Sponsorship | > | Phase 2:<br>Ethnic<br>Enclaves | > | Phase 3:<br>Assimilation |

Spontaneous International Migration (SIM): The Vietnamese Pattern

| Phase 1:<br>The<br>Homeland | > | Phase 2:<br>Ethnic<br>Enclaves | > | Phase 3:<br>Assimilation |

Asian Immigration: The Chinese and Japanese Pattern

59

*Phase 1: The Homeland.* We reason that the sociohistorical influence of the French, and later the Americans, upon the Vietnamese gives the refugees a distinct advantage over earlier Asian immigrants to the United States. Previous familiarity with Western culture, including language, employment, customs, and traditions, while limited, gives the Vietnamese a distinct kind of anticipatory socialization to the Western world. Thus when the Vietnamese leave their homeland, they have an advantage over earlier Chinese and Japanese immigrants who did not have the same familiarity with Western culture. The typical Vietnamese refugee is relatively well-educated and generally enjoyed middle class financial and career status. Often one member of a refugee family has known or worked with Americans in Vietnam (Kelly, 1977). The joint influence of these socioeconomic factors and the personal relationship with Americans facilitates the Vietnamese adaptation to America.

Phase 1 for the earlier Asian immigrants represents a time of some dissatisfaction, preparation, and then emigration from the homeland. Most who emigrate are men who leave home for financial reasons, planning to return after accumulating a nest egg (Bonacich, 1973; Kitano, 1976; Lyman, 1974).

*Phase 1a: Temporary Camps.* After leaving the homeland, the Vietnamese arrive at temporary camps in the United States. Having endured the trauma of escape and separation from loved ones, they now experience culture shock due to a new milieu—unfamiliar housing, food, and climate. While there is very limited contact at this time with the larger American society (Liu and Muratta, 1978a), this relatively brief period of camp life (a matter of a few months) does provide a transitional period for the Vietnamese which earlier Asian immigrants did not have. It is a time for the refugee to get his feet on the ground again while physical necessities such as food, shelter, and medical care are provided.

An educational program provides English language training. A further introduction to American culture is available via movies, educational films, television, and recreational programs. While many Vietnamese feel a general psychological depression over what they have left behind as well as anxiety over what the future might bring, at the same time they are now expecting to enjoy a higher life status in America than they have ever known before (Liu and Muratta, 1978b).

*Phase 1b: Private Sponsorship.* The Vietnamese next enter a period in which they are assigned to a private sponsor who pledges personal and financial support to the refugee families. From one perspective, this sponsorship period serves to disperse the Vietnamese to the four winds and deprives them of the social and psychological comfort of their ethnic community (Tran Tuong Nhu, 1976). From another perspective, this sponsorship period may provide a degree of American social contact and economic security, unknown to earlier Asian immigrants, which accelerates the pace of their assimilation. During this phase the refugees benefit from continuing public assistance to meet many of their social, psychological, and financial needs. They are assured housing and employment aid and other assistance to ease their assimilation into American society.

*Phase 2: Ethnic Enclaves.* We suspect that many Vietnamese refugees will form ethnic enclaves in large cities across America. The Vietnamese appear to be following the route taken by the Chinese and Japanese immigrant groups who came to this country in the late 19th and 20th Centuries. These earlier Asians relied heavily on ethnic group solidarity. Subsequently they made substantial social and economic achievements (Light, 1972; Lyman, 1974; Miyamoto, 1939). Since early 1976 the Vietnamese have been regrouping in recognition of their need for physical and emotional support. They have been moving from small towns to large metropolitan areas, forming ethnic communities in such cities as New York, Dallas, New Orleans, San Francisco, and Los Angeles (Kelly, 1977).

Phase 2 for the earlier Chinese and Japanese immigrants is a period in which they organized into ethnic enclaves for mutual comfort and support (Ichihashi, 1932; Kitano, 1976; Lyman, 1974). The ethnic enclaves allow the immigrants to turn inward in order to avoid a sometimes severely hostile host society (Miyamoto, 1939). The Japanese immigrants in particular maintain a sojourner orientation through most of Phase 2 (Bonacich, 1973). That is, they retain close ties to relatives in their native country and intend to return to their homeland after acquiring a measure of financial security. Thus, while being a positive step in many ways, Phase 2 for the earlier Asian immigrant is also a time of impeded or delayed socioeconomic adaptation.

*Phase 3: Assimilation.* We suspect that the Vietnamese will not embrace the ethnic enclave to the degree exhibited by earlier Asian American immigrants. For one reason, the Vietnamese refugees have not met with the severe hostility and blatant discrimination earlier Asian groups encountered. While the Vietnamese did find some hostility, as noted earlier, the fact that thousands of Americans were willing to act as sponsors indicates that there were many Americans who welcomed the Vietnamese. Because of this relatively short-lived period of ghettoization, we reason that the Vietnamese language, culture, and tradition may be more quickly eroded especially as the Vietnamese adapt socioeconomically. Indeed, we suspect that many Vietnamese will not be drawn to the ethnic enclave at all, but upon achieving greater proficiency in the English language will move headlong into Phase 3: complete socioeconomic adaptation and assimilation into the larger American society.[1]

Phase 3 for the earlier Asian immigrant also represents total and complete assimilation into American society. In terms of a developmental process, we suggest that the Chinese and Japanese by and large are approaching Phase 3 (Kitano, 1976:6). They are experiencing a measurable degree of upward mobility, with much support provided by the ethnic community (Kitano, 1976; Weiss, 1974).

We have illustrated a sociohistorical model of the Vietnamese experience which we term Spontaneous International Migration. This pattern is different from earlier Asian immigration patterns because of the Vietnamese' unique background and circumstances of migration. As the model suggests, we see rapid movement through each phase from homeland (Phase 1), to temporary camp life (Phase 1a), to sponsorship (Phase 1b), to ethnic enclave (Phase 2), and finally to complete assimilation (Phase 3). Although the Vietnamese may move through more phases of migration and resettlement than have other Asian groups (Figure 5.1), we suspect that the Vietnamese will progress through each phase more rapidly and will reach complete assimilation more quickly than have other Asian groups.

Studying the SIM model, we observe that many Vietnamese are now between Phases 2 and 3. That is, there is some regrouping of the Vietnamese into ethnic enclaves in cities as diverse as New Orleans, Los Angeles, and San Francisco. If this regrouping results in full scale ghettoization, this process will preserve the Vietnamese language, religion, and culture and will tend to extend the length of time before the Vietnamese move on to full assimilation (Phase 3). A second scenario suggests that we may witness simply a token movement into ethnic enclaves, a stay that is short-lived. If this occurs, given the high levels of employment among the Vietnamese, their increasing English language proficiency, and the relatively high proportion who profess Christianity, we will see relatively rapid assimilation. As other studies of racial and cultural minorities have shown, intermarriage will be the final barrier to full-scale assimilation of the Vietnamese into American society (Gordon, 1964; Montero, 1978b).

*Limitations of the model.* All theoretical models have inherent limitations as a product of their basic assumptions. Models necessarily are heuristic devices that are useful in summarizing a vast amount of data. The central limitations of the SIM model center around the need for more data as well as a longer time frame. Although we have based our model upon data from a national probability sample of Vietnamese refugees, these data represent only one basis upon which to build a model. Ideally, several sets of data obtained from different investigators with varying perspectives should be used to examine the model. Moreover, there is a need for more time to elapse from the point when the Vietnamese refugees first set foot on American soil. That is, we would like to collect data after an entire generation of Vietnamese has been reared in the American milieu.

## SUMMARY

In the present chapter we have seen that the pattern of Vietnamese migration fits into the larger migration literature, and yet, also possesses its own uniqueness. Thus we have developed a model of that distinct experience which we term Spontaneous International Migration (SIM). We used two types of evidence: interview data and systematic observation of the adjustment of Vietnamese to American society. In order to assess the precise accuracy of the SIM model, further studies of Vietnamese refugees are needed. In the next and final chapter we provide an overview of our central findings and place them within a broader context to provide a prognosis for the future of the Vietnamese in America.

## NOTES

1. Our use of the term "assimilation" is based upon the work of Milton Gordon (1964;1975).

# Chapter 6

# Vietnamese In America:
# Some Future Prospects

A central objective of this volume has been to analyze and document one of the most unique yet tragic migrations in human history. A second objective has been to develop a model of Spontaneous International Migration (SIM), which attempts to place the Vietnamese immigration experience in a broader sociohistorical context. The Indochinese refugees who came to America in 1975 constitute the largest single refugee group ever to arrive in the United States in such a brief period of time. They faced numerous problems upon their arrival. The very term refugee implies traumatic upheaval and the wrench of sudden separation from familiar surroundings. Psychologically they were unprepared to start life in a new country. Moreover, they had no indigenous ethnic community within the United States to give them emotional and material support. Many had been separated from other family members, a painful experience for anyone, but particularly so for the family-oriented Vietnamese. Difficulties with the English language exacerbated all their other problems.

Chapter One provided an introduction to the 1975 migration of Vietnamese to the United States. Due to a combination of factors, there is a paucity of literature on the Vietnamese in America. We reviewed the small literature which is presently available, however, in order to lay the groundwork for our present study.

In Chapter Two we briefly scanned the long history of Vietnam in order to gain a better understanding of recent events which led to the mass exodus of refugees in 1975. Beginning with the legends of prehistory, we reviewed a thousand years of Chinese rule, nine hundred years of independence, and more than three centuries of European influence. Vietnam officially became a French colony in 1883, a status which lasted until World War II. After the war France struggled to regain control of her colony, but with the fall of Dien Bien Phu in 1954, the independence of Vietnam was assured. The Geneva Agreements which ended the French-Indochina War created serious problems, however. By those agreements, Vietnam was divided along the 17th parallel. The northern part of the country was to be led by the Communist government of Ho Chi Minh, while the south went to the Nationalist, anti-Communist government of Ngo Dinh Diem. Each side claimed to be the only legitimate government of Vietnam, and the two were soon locked in a struggle for control of the entire nation.

When the United States became involved in that struggle, they first provided only financial support and military advisors to the government of South Vietnam. By 1966, however, the U.S. role had grown to full-scale military involvement. After many frustrating and confusing years of warfare, the United States withdrew all military and civilian personnel from Vietnam, and the capital of Saigon fell to the Communists in April 1975. Thousands of refugees began to flee South Vietnam, a movement which continues to the present day.

In Chapter Three we looked at a demographic profile of the Vietnamese refugees in order to discover who fled their country and why. We discovered a relatively youthful group, evenly divided between males and females. Many were among the intellectual, political, and social elite in Vietnam, and great numbers fled as members of large family groups. A disproportionate number were Catholics, a religion which includes only 10 percent of the population of Vietnam. Chapter Three also described the resettlement camps and discussed the role of the voluntary agencies in placing refugees with sponsors.

Chapter Four reported upon data collected under the auspices of HEW. The sample was based upon a population of some 35,000 Vietnamese refugees. The data provided socioeconomic profiles of a random sample of Vietnamese refugees collected over five points in time from July 1975 to August 1977. In general, the findings indicated an improving socioeconomic status among Vietnamese in America.

*Current Socioeconomic Status.* The single most telling factor about the Vietnamese' chances for finding economic self-sufficiency is their employment rate. Although there has been a good deal of downward occupational mobility among the Vietnamese refugees, as measured by their original status in Vietnam, we see very high levels of employment among them. From the time of survey one in July-August 1975 to the time of survey five in July-August 1977, the employment picture improved steadily for the Vietnamese. The employment rates for males increased from 68.2 percent to 95.1 percent. By the time of survey five, the employment rate for females nearly matched that of males, showing an increase from 50.9 percent at survey one to 93.2 percent at survey five. Recently, rates of unemployment among the Vietnamese refugees have fallen below the national average. While it is true that many of the former refugees are underemployed or work at entry-level jobs, the very fact that such a great percentage are employed bodes well for their future prospects in the United States.

Data on household income show a steady improvement from survey one through survey five. Not only are more Vietnamese working full time, they are also earning more money. The proportion of households with an income of less than $200 a month decreased from 42.1 percent in survey one to 3.2 percent in survey five. At the same time, the proportion of households with an income of $800 or more per month increased from 14.9 percent to 51.4 percent.

The Vietnamese clearly are assuming more and more responsibility for their own finances. Remember that these immigrants are relatively well educated and two-thirds are from white-collar backgrounds in Vietnam. Then too, they have had the benefit of a unique, comprehensive, and costly resettlement program, never before available to immigrant groups in the United States. This resettlement process included programs designed to provide health care, housing assistance, and a refugee sponsorship network. Survey five indicates that the largest component of household income (90.8 percent) comes from wages and salaries. Federal assistance and other financial contributions represent a declining portion of total household income. Thus the Vietnamese who fled to America in 1975 appear to be moving steadily toward economic self-sufficiency and are carving a permanent niche for themselves in American society.

From survey one through survey five, limited English proficiency appears to have become less of a problem for the Vietnamese. With exposure to other Americans and the mass media and with Vietnamese children attending American schools, it seems only a matter of time until the great majority of Vietnamese in the United States are functionally fluent in English.

In Chapter Five we presented a sociohistorical model of Spontaneous International Migration (SIM) comparing the immigration experience of the Vietnamese with earlier Asian immigrants in America. While the earlier Asian Americans appear to have passed through fewer phases than the Vietnamese while moving toward assimilation, it is possible that the Vietnamese may assimilate more quickly than have earlier Asian immigrants because of the refugees' unique background and greater degree of anticipatory socialization. The precise applicability of the model to the Vietnamese immigration experience will perhaps have to wait until more time has elapsed during the resettlement process. We can then better determine whether the Vietnamese do indeed move from Phase 1 to Phase 3 more rapidly than have other Asian immigrants, or even newer immigrants such as the Cubans. Clearly, future studies are needed.

## THE CONTINUING STRUGGLE

To be a refugee is to seek refuge. The Vietnamese who fled to the United States appear to have found safety. Have they also found a path toward financial and emotional security? Many indications are that the answer is yes. The quest is far from over, however. Struggling to become economically self-sufficient, many Vietnamese find themselves working in lower-level jobs with little remuneration or opportunity for advancement. Many were members of Vietnam's educational, urban elite, and their drop in occupational status and loss of prestige in some cases may have contributed to an emotional crisis. Indeed, one of the most compelling problems faced by the refugees is psychological depression.

In addition to the occupational factors cited above, some Vietnamese have also attributed this depression to the knowledge that South Vietnam is now governed by Communists. Many are worried about reports of abuse and torture in Vietnam. They fear they will never be able to return to their homeland, and agonize over friends and relatives left behind. The emotional problems the refugees are experiencing will hopefully be ameliorated with the scheduled training of paraprofessionals who are sensitive to the cultural needs of the Vietnamese.

Besides the usual difficulties associated with job-seeking which might have been expected, the Vietnamese have faced an additional problem. They arrived in the United States during a period of economic recession and high unemployment, leading some Americans to react with open hostility to an influx of refugees which they feared would create added competition in a dwindling job market.

Those Americans who did welcome the refugees were inexperienced in coping with such large numbers of unexpected immigrants. Refugee camps were a new phenomenon in the United States. The government had an enormous task in coordinating the many government and voluntary agencies to work efficiently, as well as humanely, with the refugees. The pressure to empty the camps quickly and the policy of dispersing the refugees throughout the states contributed to resettlement problems. Many Americans who became sponsors were naive about the many difficulties they would face, and refugees themselves often had unrealistic expectations about life in America.

CHANGE IN STATUS

When the Vietnamese first arrived in the United States, they were admitted without visas as parolees due to the emergency nature of their situation. It soon became evident that legislation was required to give the refugees greater access to educational and vocational opportunities than their parolee status allowed. Public Law 95-145, based on similar legislation directed toward

69

Cuban refugees in 1966, went into effect on October 28, 1977. This law changes the status of the Vietnamese refugee from parolee to permanent resident alien. It provides a retroactive period of residence so that all the time spent in the United States since March 1975 counts toward the five years' residency required to become a naturalized citizen (Hohl, 1978; U.S. Department of Health, Education, and Welfare, 1977d). The parolees must apply for this change of status, and the voluntary agencies are working closely with the U.S. Immigration and Naturalization Service to expedite the processing of these applicants.

## THE BOAT PEOPLE

The resettlement of those refugees who fled Vietnam in 1975 is not the end of the refugee story. After the fall of Saigon to the Communists in April 1975, small groups of people continued to flee their country. Some escaped overland, making their way to refugee camps in Thailand. The Thai government has been placed in the awkward position of trying not to provoke the Communist nations which border her, while providing a safe haven for the desperate refugees. The Thais thus are extremely eager for other countries to receive the refugees who continue to enter Thailand (Hohl, 1978).

Other small groups have left Vietnam in tiny fishing vessels or small craft never intended for use on the open seas. These became the so-called boat people whose dramatic plight the world community has not been able to overlook. This movement of boat people started as a trickle in 1975 but increased to vast proportions in the fall of 1978. More than 85,000 boat people, it is estimated, fled Vietnam in the last months of 1978 (Weintraub, 1978). As the Communist regime in Vietnam tightened its reins and began instituting far-reaching social reforms, thousands of Chinese merchants faced the confiscation of their businesses. Unable or unwilling to adjust to agricultural or communal living, they left Vietnam. Sixty percent of the boat people are these ethnic Chinese (Chapman, 1978a).

The boat people who survived disease, hunger, drowning, and piracy found themselves unwanted and often forced back to sea when they reached the coast of Malaysia. Hundreds have drowned at sea within sight of land, having been turned away by Malaysian authorities or angry villagers. Malaysia is a poor country, ill equipped to accept thousands of refugees. While the United Nations provides goods for the refugees, Malaysia must police and transport those refugees who land on her shores. The government of Malaysia has angrily denounced those nations who simply contribute money toward the refugee problem. Rather, Malaysia urgently seeks wide-scale settlement of the refugees in those nations which she views as most responsible for their existence.

It is not known for sure the exact number of boat people who have fled Vietnam, but by late 1978 many tens of thousands were living in primitive camps, some lacking even a reliable fresh water supply. Since 1975 the United States has authorized the admittance of increasing numbers of boat people, over and above immigrant quotas. United States' action regarding the refugees, however, has been termed completely inadequate by Malaysian authorities. Clearly, the refugee problem is one which faces not only the United States, but the entire world community.

A report prepared for the use of the Committee on the Judiciary, United States Senate, summarizes the problem:

> The humanitarian needs of war victims continue in Vietnam and Laos. Severe and growing food shortages in these countries threaten famine conditions in some areas and the health and well-being of many people—especially in Laos. Some 100,000 displaced persons from the Indochina Peninsula are present in Thailand, and the number is growing every day. Thousands of "boat people" from Vietnam are present in many countries of Asia, and, again, the number is growing every day. In short, critical humanitarian problems are facing the countries of Southeast Asia. A new regional crisis of people is building—in the aftermath of the Indochina War.
>
> In the recent past, it has been easy for the United States to pick and choose who we should help and how we should help. But we should abandon this piecemeal approach and develop more comprehensive policies and programs, that more realistically respond to the interrelated humanitarian problems of the entire area (U.S., Congress, Senate, 1978:39).

Specifically, the report further recommends: (1) normalization of relations with Vietnam, (2) contribution of food and humanitarian assistance to Vietnam and Laos, (3) recognition of the United States' continuing responsibility to admit Indochinese refugees, (4) development of a more balanced American policy toward the refugee problem in Southeast Asia, and (5) promo-

71

tion of the involvement of the international community in this on-going problem.

## FUTURE STUDY

The study of the Indochinese refugees has just begun. Clearly, the data presented in this volume simply lay the groundwork for future study. Given the paucity of research on refugee populations, it is clear that the original Vietnamese respondents in our sample should be reinterviewed annually, thus ensuring that this rich and unique sample of Vietnamese is not lost to professional and lay audiences. This project would be relatively low in cost and easy to effectuate. The sample survey would allow for studies of geographic mobility, differential levels of assimilation by generation, as well as the changing socioeconomic status of the refugees. Additionally, a five-year follow-up on the Vietnamese refugees to determine their progress over time could prove of great value in understanding mass migrations and their effects on both the refugees and their host countries.

The Spontaneous International Migration of the Vietnamese in 1975 could become the most well-documented refugee movement in history. Recent events in Southeast Asia often have had tragic consequences for those forced to flee their native lands. As more and more refugees continue to arrive in the United States, the lessons learned from the 1975 migration may well serve the needs of future refugees.

# Appendix A

Chronology of Events: The American Withdrawal from Vietnam and the Vietnamese Resettlement in the United States

1975

| | |
|---|---|
| April 8 through April 15 | State Department officials consult with House and Senate Committees regarding use of Attorney General's "parole" authority for evacuees from Indochina. |
| April 12 | U.S. Embassy, Phnom Penh closes. Last Americans are evacuated in operation "Eagle Pull." |
| April 12 through April 17 | U.S. Mission, Geneva asked to request assistance from United Nations High Commissioner for Refugees (UNHCR) and Intergovernmental Committee for European Migration (ICEM) in locating third countries willing to accept refugees from Indochina. |
| April 14 | Parole is authorized for dependents of American citizens currently in Vietnam. |

73

| April 18 | The President asks twelve Federal agencies "to coordinate . . . all U.S. Government activities concerning evacuation of U.S. citizens, Vietnamese citizens, and third country nationals from Vietnam and refugee resettlement problems relating to the Vietnam conflict" and names Ambassador L. Dean Brown as his Special Representative and Director of the Special Interagency Task Force. |
| --- | --- |
| April 19 | Parole is extended to include categories of relatives of American citizens or permanent resident aliens who are petition holders. |
| April 22 | The Interagency Task Force asks civil and military authorities on Guam to prepare a safe haven estimated to be required for 90 days in order to provide care and maintenance for an estimated 50,000 refugees. The first to pass through the area arrive the following day. |
| April 25 | The Attorney General authorizes parole for additional categories of relatives, Cambodians in third countries and up to 50,000 "high-risk" Vietnamese. |
| April 27 | The Task Force requests all American missions overseas to take up the possible resettlement of refugees as a matter of urgency. |
| April 29 | U.S. Embassy, Saigon, closes. Operation Frequent Wind removes last Americans and Vietnamese by helicopter from staging sites in Saigon. The sea-lift and self-evacuation continue. Camp Pendleton, California opens as a refugee center prepared to care for 18,000 refugees. |
| May 2 | Fort Chaffee, Arkansas opens as a refugee reception center prepared to care for 24,000 refugees. |
| May 4 | Eglin Air Force Base, Florida opens as a refugee reception center prepared to accept 2,500 refugees (a figure later increased to 5,000). |

| May 5 | Ambassador Brown and senior Task Force officials testify before the Senate Foreign Affairs Committee. |
|---|---|
| | Ambassador Brown and senior Task Force officials testify before the House Appropriations Defense Subcommittee in connection with the Administration's request for $507 million to run the refugee program. |
| May 7 | Ambassador Brown and senior Task Force officials testify before the Senate Judiciary Committee, the House International Relations Committee, and on May 8, the House Judiciary Committee. |
| May 22 | Ambassador Brown and senior Task Force officials testify before the House Judiciary Subcommittee. |
| | A House and Senate conference committee agrees on the language of the Indochina Migration and Refugee Assistance Act of 1975, appropriating $405 million for the Administration's refugee program. |
| May 24 | The Act becomes PL 94-23 as the President signs it into law. |
| May 27 | Ambassador Brown returns to his post at the Middle East Institute and the President asks Mrs. Julia Vadala Taft, Deputy Assistant Secretary of Health, Education, and Welfare for Human Development, to act as Director of the Interagency Task Force until arrangements are completed for organizing the Government's efforts for the longer term. |
| May 28 | A fourth Stateside reception center is opened at Fort Indiantown Gap, Pennsylvania and receives its first refugees. |
| May 29 | The UNHCR sends a representative to Stateside reception center at Fort Chaffee to interview in- |

dividuals who have indicated a desire to return to Vietnam and whose names had been furnished earlier. Representatives of the UNHCR have been working similarly on Guam for several weeks, will go to Pendleton and Indiantown Gap next week and to Eglin thereafter.

June 6  HEW establishes a special Task Force with representatives of the American Medical Association, the American Association of Medical Colleges, the Educational Commission on Foreign Medical Graduates, and a number of programs within HEW that deal with training and placement of physicians in the U.S.

June 15  The President sends a report to the Congress as required by PL 94-23.

July 5  First of a series of regional meetings with local government officials and representatives of resettlement agencies held in New York City.

July 6  Subic Bay, Philippines, refugee reception center closes.

July 21  Principal operational responsibility for the Task Force is transferred from the Department of State to the Department of Health, Education, and Welfare. Julia Vadala Taft is named as Director of the Task Force.

August 1  Wake Island reception center closes.

Attorney General extends parole authority to additional Indochina refugees stranded in "third countries."

September 15  Eglin Air Force Base, Florida refugee reception center closes.

September 23  The President transmits the Second Report to the Congress on the activities of the Interagency Task Force.

| September 30 | Decision made to accede to demands of repatriates on Guam for a ship to be sailed by them to Vietnam. |
|---|---|
| October 16 | The Vietnamese freighter, Vietnam Thuong Tin I, sails from Guam bound for Vietnam with 1,546 repatriates aboard. |
| October 31 | Last date for movement of Indochina refugees stranded in third countries into the U.S. refugee system. Henceforth, admission of refugees into the United States is the responsibility of the Department of State. |
| October 31 | UN High Commissioner for Refugees meets with Task Force and State Department officials. UNHCR agrees to accept responsibility for Cambodian refugees who do not wish to accept sponsorship offers and desire to be repatriated. |
| October 31 | Reception centers on Guam and at Camp Pendleton, California close. |
| December 15 | Indiantown Gap Military Reservation, Pennsylvania refugee reception center closes. |
| December 20 | Last 24 refugees leave Fort Chaffee resettlement center to join sponsors, and this center, the last to remain in operation, is officially closed. |
| December 31 | Interagency Task Force operations are terminated, ending first phase of refugee program—evacuation and resettlement. |

1976

| January 1 | HEW Refugee Task Force assumes responsibility for domestic resettlement. |
|---|---|
| February 6 | State Department and Attorney General's office consult with Judiciary Subcommittee on Immigration, Citizenship and International Law (Joshua Eilberg, Chairman) on issuance of parole authority to admit to the U.S. 11,000 Indochina refugees now in camps in Thailand. |

| | |
|---|---|
| February 12 | HEW Refugee Task Force and Voluntary resettlement agencies (VOLAGs) meet in Washington to examine methods for a coordinated effort to assure opportunities for self-sufficiency among the new immigrants. |
| February 18-19 | Conference for HEW Regional Refugee Assistance Coordinators held in Washington to discuss domestic resettlement priorities. |
| February 23-26 | HEW Refugee Task Force Director and Deputy Regional Director attend a series of meetings with State of California, local county officials, and a number of VOLAG executive directors to discuss refugee resettlement issues. |
| March 15 | Voluntary Agency directors sign HEW Strategy and Objectives Memorandum pledging to reduce cash assistance cases by 50 percent by October 1, 1976. |
| March 17 | House Subcommittee on HEW Appropriation meets with HEW Refugee Task Force Director to discuss FY 1977 budget. |
| March 17 | HEW Social and Rehabilitation Service establishes with the States a reporting system for Alien Registration Numbers of refugees on welfare. |
| March 31 | Seattle regional conference of HEW Task Force, voluntary agencies, State officials, refugees, and sponsors yields guidelines for joint actions. |
| April 8 | Senate Subcommittee on HEW Appropriations holds hearing on FY 1977 Refugee Task Force funding. |
| April 9 | HEW Regional Offices are directed to develop plans for using seed monies to fund local activities designed to remove refugees from the cash assistance rolls and place them in jobs. |
| May 5 | An Expanded Parole Program for 11,000 additional Cambodian, Vietnamese, and Laotian refugees is authorized by the Attorney General. |

| | |
|---|---|
| May 20-21 | Representatives from HEW's Refugee Task Force, Office of Education, and Social and Rehabilitation Service (SRS) meet to develop Federal strategies on refugee assistance for the future, including the role of Indochinese self-help groups, and on the phasing of residual Task Force responsibilities into SRS. |
| June 4 | Nationwide conference for State resettlement groups and representatives from State Governors' offices is held in Kansas City to exchange information and ideas. |
| June 4 | $2 million allocated to the State of California for a special English language and vocational training program. |
| June 4 | $400,000 allotted to Regional Offices to develop and implement job development programs for refugees. |
| June 23 | New contract set up with Center for Applied Linguistics to continue toll-free telephone service until 1977 and also to develop material and conduct training sessions in area of adult vocationally oriented English language training. |
| June 29 | Contract with the American Bar Association, Young Lawyers Section, expanded to extend toll-free telephone service for legal advice to refugees until March 1977. Also added were funds for ABA to research major legal problem areas being faced by refugees. |
| July 1 | Laotians became eligible by P.L. 94-313 for benefits bestowed by Indochina Migration and Refugee Assistance Act of 1975 on Vietnamese and Cambodians. |
| July 12 | Indochinese Mutual Assistance Division set up within HEW Refugee Task Force to provide technical assistance liaison channels for more than 100 identified refugee self-help associations throughout the country. |

| | |
|---|---|
| July 14 | Money allotted to Regional Offices to develop Mental Health Program for refugees. |
| July 21 | Conference on cash assistance eligibility requirements for refugees. Participants included representatives from HEW, VOLAGs, and state and local welfare agencies. |
| July 26 | Notice of $5 million employment and training grant availability published in Federal Register. |
| July 26-30 | Task Force visits to Regional Offices concerning $5 million employment and training grants to Regional staffs. |
| August 4 | Draft of new cash assistance policy statement mailed to appropriate groups. |
| August 31 | Applications for employment and training grants received in Regional Offices. |
| September 10 | Indochina Refugee Children Assistance Act of 1976 (P.L. 94-405) extending educational assistance for elementary-secondary students and adults for school year 1976-77. |
| September 20 | Third Wave Survey Report on Refugee Resettlement by Opportunity Systems, Inc., completed. |
| September 29 | Administrator of Social and Rehabilitation Service, Commissioner of Assistance Payments Administration, and other SRS officials meet with national VOLAG Directors in preparation for transfer of Task Force responsibilities to SRS. |
| September 30 | SRS Regional Commissioners approve 58 grants totaling $5 million for English language and vocational training and job development and placement. |
| October 1 | HEW Indochina Refugee Task Force transferred from Office of the Secretary to Social and Rehabilitation Service, Assistance Payments Administration, U.S. Repatriate and Refugee Assistance Staff. |

| October 1 | Foreign Assistance and Related Programs Appropriation Act (P.L. 94-441) appropriated the remaining $50 million of the $455 million originally authorized by the Indochina Migration and Refugee Assistance Act of 1975. It also extended the availability to HEW of all appropriated funds until September 30, 1977. |
|---|---|
| October 22 | SRS Action Transmittal to the States providing revised guidelines for cash assistance for refugees, requiring acceptance of appropriate employment or training and authorizing State welfare agencies to carry out job development activities. |
| November 10 | Completion by Task Force of initial Regional technical-assistance workshops for all employment/training project grantees. |
| December 6 | Contract awarded to Center for Applied Linguistics to provide technical assistance to employment program grantees. |

1977

| February 8 | Completion by Task Force of second round of Regional assistance workshops for all employment/training project grantees. |
|---|---|
| May 4 | Supplemental Appropriations Act (P.L. 95-26) includes $18.5 million for funds to State educational agencies to reimburse local educational agencies for services to Indochinese refugee schoolchildren and $10.25 million for discretionary project grants to State and local educational agencies for English and vocational/occupational training for adult refugees. Funds were appropriated under authority of the Indochina Refugee Children Assistance Act of 1976 (P.L. 94-405). |
| June 19 | Under HEW reorganization, Indochinese Refugee Task Force becomes part of Special Programs Staff, Office of Family Assistance, in the Social Security Administration. |

| July 15 | After studying State Department report, President Carter asks Attorney General to use parole powers to admit additional 15,000 refugees, including 7,000 "boat cases," to United States. |
| August 9-10 | Refugee Task Force and National Institute of Mental Health hold two-day conference on refugee mental health programs in Denver. |
| August 11 | Attorney General Griffin B. Bell uses parole power to authorize admission of additional 15,000 refugees, following Congressional concurrence. |
| September 20 | First 107 of 15,000 new refugees arrive in San Francisco port-of-entry after flight from Bangkok. |
| October 18 | Congress completes passage of bill phasing down refugee assistance program over four-year period and providing for adjustment of status from parolee to permanent resident alien for refugees. |
| October 28 | President approves extension and adjustment of status bill, which becomes P.L. 94-145. |

---

Source:   U.S. Department of Health, Education, and Welfare (1977d:12-20).

# Appendix B

SAMPLE COMPARISONS

TABLE B.1

COMPOSITION OF SAMPLE AND POPULATION
BY SEX

| | Population | | Initial Sample | | Unlocated Subjects | | Adjusted Sample | |
|---|---|---|---|---|---|---|---|---|
| | No. | Percent | No. | Percent | No. | Percent | No. | Percent |
| Female | 15,816 | 45.9 | 2,305 | 46.9 | 1,544 | 46.6 | 763 | 47.4 |
| Male | 16,861 | 48.9 | 2,363 | 48.0 | 1,549 | 46.7 | 814 | 50.5 |
| N/A | 1,811 | 5.3 | 256 | 5.2 | 222 | 6.7 | 34 | 2.1 |
| | 34,488 | 100.1 | 4,926 | 100.1 | 3,315 | 100.0 | 1,611 | 100.0 |

## Table B.2

### Composition of Sample and Population By Age

| Age | Population | | Initial Sample | | Unlocated Subjects | | Adjusted Sample | |
|---|---|---|---|---|---|---|---|---|
| | No. | Percent | No. | Percent | No. | Percent | No. | Percent |
| 11-13 | 10,465 | 30.3 | 1,463 | 29.7 | 1,016 | 30.7 | 447 | 27.8 |
| 14-24 | 8,703 | 25.2 | 1,298 | 26.3 | 842 | 25.4 | 456 | 28.3 |
| 25-34 | 6,098 | 17.7 | 867 | 17.6 | 562 | 17.0 | 305 | 19.0 |
| 35-44 | 3,438 | 10.0 | 491 | 10.0 | 321 | 9.7 | 170 | 10.6 |
| 45-54 | 1,621 | 4.7 | 215 | 4.4 | 129 | 3.9 | 86 | 5.3 |
| 55-64 | 817 | 2.4 | 110 | 2.2 | 69 | 2.1 | 41 | 2.5 |
| 65+ | 407 | 1.2 | 63 | 1.3 | 48 | 1.4 | 15 | 0.9 |
| N/A | 2,939 | 8.5 | 419 | 8.5 | 328 | 9.8 | 91 | 5.6 |
| | 34,488 | 100.0 | 4,926 | 100.0 | 3,315 | 100.0 | 1,611 | 100.0 |

## Table B.3

### Composition of Sample and Population By Educational Attainment

| Education | Population | | Initial Sample | | Unlocated Subjects | | Adjusted Sample | |
|---|---|---|---|---|---|---|---|---|
| | No. | Percent | No. | Percent | No. | Percent | No. | Percent |
| Elementary | 3,806 | 11.1 | 567 | 11.5 | 424 | 12.8 | 143 | 8.9 |
| Secondary | 7,438 | 21.5 | 1,090 | 22.1 | 678 | 20.5 | 412 | 25.6 |
| University | 3,322 | 9.7 | 462 | 9.4 | 273 | 8.2 | 189 | 11.7 |
| Postgraduate | 768 | 2.2 | 94 | 1.9 | 64 | 1.9 | 30 | 1.9 |
| N/A | 19,154 | 55.5 | 2,713 | 55.1 | 1,876 | 56.6 | 837 | 51.9 |
| | 34,488 | 100.0 | 4,926 | 100.0 | 3,315 | 100.0 | 1,611 | 100.0 |

84

## TABLE B.4

### COMPOSITION OF SAMPLE AND POPULATION
### BY TIME OF RELEASE FROM CAMP

| Time of Release | Population | | Initial Sample | | Unlocated Subjects | | Adjusted Sample | |
|---|---|---|---|---|---|---|---|---|
| | No. | Percent | No. | Percent | No. | Percent | No. | Percent |
| May | 6,737 | 19.5 | 966 | 19.6 | 697 | 21.0 | 269 | 16.7 |
| June | 18,359 | 53.2 | 2,630 | 53.4 | 1,762 | 53.1 | 868 | 53.8 |
| July | 9,039 | 26.2 | 1,285 | 26.1 | 819 | 24.7 | 466 | 29.0 |
| August | 232 | 0.7 | 30 | 0.6 | 22 | 0.7 | 8 | 0.5 |
| N/A | 121 | 0.4 | 15 | 0.3 | 15 | 0.5 | – | — |
| | 34,488 | 100.0 | 4,926 | 100.0 | 3,315 | 100.0 | 1,611 | 100.0 |

# Appendix C

Supplemental Tables[1]

The tables which follow have been photographically reproduced from the five wave reports. (See Opportunity Systems, Inc., 1975; 1976a; 1976b; 1977a; 1977b.) Given the number of tables which were generated by the five wave surveys, it was impossible to include more than a few tables in the body of this volume. Therefore, I have provided these tables as raw data for scholars who may wish to do further analysis.

The table numbering system refers to the appendix, the survey number, and the table number. For example, C.5.1. refers to Appendix C, survey 5, table 1. Thus this numbering system facilitates cross referencing to related material in the text.

---

1. In reporting the data in the tables which follow, Opportunity Systems, Inc., follows some rather unconventional techniques of which the reader should be aware. The total number of cases indicated on some tables exceeds the total number actually reported there. For example, when 1,000 respondents were interviewed, 1,000 is reported as the grand total although the responses recorded in the breakdown may equal only 990. This difference reflects individuals who did not respond to that particular question. Total percentages are all reported as 100 percent although, again, the breakdown of the percentages may not equal precisely 100 percent. These differences may generally be attributed to rounding errors.

TABLE C.1.1

LABOR FORCE PARTICIPATION OF PERSONS 14 YEARS AND OLDER
BY SEX AND RELATIONSHIP TO HEADS OF HOUSEHOLD
(WEIGHTED PERCENTAGES)

| Relationship to Heads of Household | Male | | | Female | | |
|---|---|---|---|---|---|---|
| | Unweighted N | In Labor Force | Not In Labor Force | Unweighted N | In Labor Force | Not In Labor Force |
| Total . . . . . . . | 2,866 | 69.0 | 31.0 | 2,994 | 39.3 | 60.7 |
| Head . . . . . . . | 1,251 | 87.2 | 12.8 | 291 | 62.7 | 37.3 |
| Spouse . . . . . . | 57 | 62.2 | 37.8 | 1,034 | 35.5 | 64.5 |
| Child or spouse . | 765 | 40.0 | 60.0 | 800 | 33.3 | 66.7 |
| Grandchild/nephew/ niece . . . . . | 99 | 50.0 | 50.0 | 88 | 34.4 | 65.6 |
| Parent or spouse . | 76 | 27.9 | 72.1 | 218 | 6.8 | 93.2 |
| Other relative . | 581 | 61.8 | 38.2 | 537 | 45.2 | 54.8 |
| Unrelated/NA . . | 37 | 28.0 | 72.0 | 26 | 48.6 | 51.6 |

TABLE C.1.2

EMPLOYMENT STATUS OF PERSONS 14 YEARS AND OLDER
BY SEX AND RELATIONSHIP TO HEADS OF HOUSEHOLD
(WEIGHTED PERCENTAGES)

| Relationship to Heads of Household | Male | | | Female | | |
|---|---|---|---|---|---|---|
| | Un-weighted N | Employed | Un-Employed | Un-weighted N | Employed | Un-Employed |
| Total . . . . . . | 1,887 | 68.2 | 31.8 | 1,122 | 50.9 | 49.1 |
| Head . . . . . . | 1,110 | 68.1 | 31.9 | 194 | 53.7 | 46.3 |
| Spouse . . . . . | 38 | 63.0 | 37.0 | 352 | 46.2 | 53.8 |
| Child or spouse . | 303 | 67.5 | 32.5 | 276 | 52.9 | 47.1 |
| Grandchild/nephew/niece . . . . . | 44 | 70.6 | 29.4 | 28 | 51.5 | 48.5 |
| Parent or spouse | 21 | 54.1 | 45.9 | 16 | 27.9 | 72.1 |
| Other relative . | 356 | 69.1 | 30.9 | 244 | 55.1 | 44.9 |
| Unrelated/NA . . | 15 | 50.0 | 50.0 | 12 | 53.1 | 46.9 |

TABLE C.1.3

EMPLOYMENT STATUS OF PERSONS 14 YEARS AND OLDER
BY VOLAG
(WEIGHTED PERCENTAGES)

| VOLAG | Unweighted N | Employed | Unemployed |
|---|---|---|---|
| Total . . . . . . . . . . . | 3,024 | 61.9 | 38.1 |
| Church World Service . . . . | 352 | 61.5 | 38.5 |
| IRC . . . . . . . . . | 549 | 52.6 | 47.4 |
| Lutheran Service . . . . . | 533 | 73.0 | 27.0 |
| Tolstoy Foundation . . . . | 83 | 48.8 | 51.2 |
| United HIAS Service . . . . | 107 | 76.1 | 23.9 |
| U.S.C.C. . . . . . . . | 1,019 | 61.5 | 38.5 |
| Other . . . . . . . . | 242 | 66.5 | 33.5 |
| No VOLAG . . . . . . | 139 | 54.4 | 45.6 |

TABLE C.1.4

EMPLOYMENT STATUS OF PERSONS 14 YEARS AND OLDER
BY LENGTH OF TIME SINCE DEPARTURE FROM CAMP
(WEIGHTED PERCENTAGES)

| Length of Time Since Departure from Camp | Unweighted N | Employed | Unemployed |
|---|---|---|---|
| Total . . . . . . . . . . . . | 3,017 | 61.9 | 38.1 |
| Less than 1 month . . . . . | 4 | – | – |
| 1 month or more but less than 2 months . . . . . . . . | 180 | 65.6 | 34.4 |
| 2 months or more but less than 3 months . . . . . . . . | 1,464 | 62.2 | 37.8 |
| 3 months or more . . . . . | 1,369 | 61.1 | 38.9 |

## TABLE C.1.5

### EMPLOYMENT STATUS OF PERSONS 14 YEARS AND OLDER
### BY AGE AND SEX
### (WEIGHTED PERCENTAGES)

| Age | Male | | | Female | | |
|---|---|---|---|---|---|---|
| | Un-weighted N | Employed | Un-Employed | Un-weighted N | Employed | Un-Employed |
| Total . . . . . . | 1,888 | 68.2 | 31.8 | 1,120 | 50.9 | 49.1 |
| 14-24 . . . . . | 550 | 64.2 | 35.8 | 446 | 51.5 | 48.5 |
| 25-34 . . . . . | 578 | 75.6 | 24.4 | 406 | 51.0 | 49.0 |
| 35-44 . . . . . | 451 | 71.0 | 29.0 | 205 | 53.2 | 46.8 |
| 45-54 . . . . . | 246 | 59.2 | 40.8 | 50 | 44.5 | 55.5 |
| 55-over . . . . | 63 | 24.4 | 75.6 | 13 | 29.4 | 70.6 |

## TABLE C.1.6

### EMPLOYMENT STATUS OF PERSONS 14 YEARS AND OLDER
### BY SEX AND EDUCATIONAL ATTAINMENT
### (WEIGHTED PERCENTAGES)

| Education | Male | | | Female | | |
|---|---|---|---|---|---|---|
| | Unweighted N | Employed | Unemployed | Unweighted N | Employed | Unemployed |
| Total | 1,989 | 68.2 | 31.8 | 1,181 | 50.9 | 49.1 |
| None | 103 | 56.0 | 44.0 | 137 | 37.0 | 63.0 |
| Primary Diploma | 85 | 72.0 | 28.0 | 99 | 55.0 | 45.0 |
| BEPSI/DEPSI/BE | 317 | 68.0 | 32.0 | 294 | 55.0 | 45.0 |
| BACC I | 188 | 65.0 | 35.0 | 129 | 51.0 | 49.0 |
| BACC II | 684 | 73.0 | 27.0 | 326 | 51.0 | 49.0 |
| University | 487 | 64.0 | 36.0 | 152 | 53.0 | 47.0 |
| Other | 49 | 53.0 | 47.0 | 9 | - | - |

Primary Diploma:
Elementary school diploma, awarded to those who pass an examination after
five years of schooling, from grade one through grade five.

BEPSI/DEPSI/BE:
Junior high school diploma, awarded to those who pass an examination after
their completion of the ninth grade.

BACC I and BACC II:
(Baccalaureate--1st part and 2nd part, respectively): awarded to those who
have successfully completed their 11th and 12th grades in secondary school;
generally considered as the main criteria in the selection of candidates for
mid-level positions in the government. BACC II (Baccalaureate--2nd part)
is a prerequisite for admission into college or university.

## TABLE C.1.7

### EMPLOYMENT STATUS OF PERSONS 14 YEARS AND OLDER BY PROFICIENCY IN ENGLISH
### (WEIGHTED PERCENTAGES)

| Proficiency in English | Unweighted N | Employed | Unemployed |
|---|---|---|---|
| Total . . . . . . . . | 3,224 | 61.9 | 38.1 |
| Understand English | | | |
| Not at all . . . . | 129 | 61.4 | 38.6 |
| Some . . . . . . | 1,882 | 59.2 | 40.8 |
| Well . . . . . . . | 975 | 66.9 | 33.1 |
| Speak English | | | |
| Not at all . . . . | 143 | 58.5 | 41.5 |
| Some . . . . . . | 1,989 | 59.3 | 40.7 |
| Well . . . . . . . | 946 | 67.3 | 32.7 |
| Read English | | | |
| Not at all . . . . | 144 | 56.3 | 43.7 |
| Some . . . . . . | 1,817 | 60.2 | 39.8 |
| Well . . . . . . . | 1,024 | 65.3 | 34.7 |
| Write English | | | |
| Not at all . . . . | 158 | 57.1 | 42.9 |
| Some . . . . . . | 1,837 | 60.2 | 39.8 |
| Well . . . . . . . | 991 | 65.6 | 34.4 |

## TABLE C.1.8

### LABOR FORCE PARTICIPATION OF PERSONS 14 YEARS AND OLDER BY PROFICIENCY IN ENGLISH
#### (WEIGHTED PERCENTAGES)

| Proficiency in English | Unweighted N | In Labor Force | | Not in Labor Force |
|---|---|---|---|---|
| | | Employed | Unemployed | |
| Total . . . . . . . . | 5,879 | 33.7 | 20.7 | 45.6 |
| Understand English | | | | |
| Not at all . . . | 636 | 12.4 | 7.8 | 79.6 |
| Some . . . . . | 3,784 | 30.9 | 21.3 | 47.8 |
| Well . . . . | 1,300 | 51.6 | 25.4 | 23.0 |
| Speak English | | | | |
| Not at all . . . | 669 | 12.7 | 9.0 | 78.3 |
| Some . . . . . | 3,782 | 31.2 | 21.4 | 47.4 |
| Well . . . . | 1,272 | 51.6 | 25.1 | 23.3 |
| Read English | | | | |
| Not at all . . . | 687 | 11.9 | 9.2 | 78.9 |
| Some . . . . . | 3,671 | 31.2 | 20.6 | 48.2 |
| Well . . . . | 1,385 | 50.5 | 26.7 | 22.8 |
| Write English | | | | |
| Not at all . . . | 717 | 12.8 | 9.5 | 77.7 |
| Some . . . . . | 3,682 | 31.5 | 20.8 | 47.7 |
| Well . . . . | 1,321 | 50.4 | 26.4 | 23.2 |

## TABLE C.1.9

### EMPLOYMENT STATUS OF HEADS OF HOUSEHOLD
### BY VIETNAM OCCUPATION
### (WEIGHTED PERCENTAGES)

| Vietnam Occupation | Unweighted N | Employed | Unemployed |
|---|---|---|---|
| Total . . . . | 1,262 | 65.4 | 34.6 |
| Professional . . . | 389 | 68.3 | 31.7 |
| Managers . . . | 423 | 67.6 | 32.4 |
| Sales . . . | 23 | 50.0 | 50.0 |
| Clerical . . . | 230 | 63.4 | 36.6 |
| Craftsmen . . . | 98 | 62.6 | 37.4 |
| Operative . . . | 11 | 91.8 | 8.2 |
| Transport . . . | 16 | 85.7 | 14.3 |
| Laborers . . . | 41 | 72.1 | 27.9 |
| Other Service . . | 16 | 80.0 | 20.0 |
| Farmers . . . | 5 | – | – |
| Farm Laborers | 1 | – | – |

TABLE C.1.10

PRESENT EMPLOYMENT OF HEADS OF HOUSEHOLD COMPARED TO
VIETNAM OCCUPATION BY VOLAG
(WEIGHTED PERCENTAGES)

| VOLAG | Unweighted N | Under-employed | Employed at Comparable Occupation Level | Employed at Higher Occupation Level |
|---|---|---|---|---|
| Total . . . . . . . . . | 1,451 | 76.0 | 19.5 | 4.5 |
| Church World Service . | 151 | 73.5 | 21.9 | 4.6 |
| IRC (International Rescue Committee) . . | 226 | 78.8 | 17.2 | 4.0 |
| Lutheran Immigration and Refugee Service . | 257 | 75.9 | 19.5 | 4.6 |
| United HIAS Service . . | 74 | 77.0 | 21.6 | 1.4 |
| U.S.C.C. . . . . . . . | 536 | 79.5 | 15.3 | 5.2 |
| Other . . . . . . . . | 153 | 76.5 | 19.6 | 3.9 |
| No VOLAG . . . . . . . | 54 | 37.0 | 59.3 | 3.7 |

97

TABLE C.1.11

PRESENT EMPLOYMENT OF HEADS OF HOUSEHOLD COMPARED TO
VIETNAM OCCUPATION BY TYPES OF SPONSOR
(WEIGHTED PERCENTAGES)

| Types of Sponsor | Unweighted N | Under-employed | Employed at Comparable Occupation Level | Employed at Higher Occupation Level |
|---|---|---|---|---|
| Total . . . . . . . . . | 852 | 76.0 | 19.5 | 4.5 |
| Individual . . . . . . . . | 130 | 73.5 | 21.4 | 5.1 |
| Family . . . . . . . . | 426 | 76.6 | 19.5 | 3.8 |
| Group . . . . . . . . | 285 | 76.7 . | 17.9 | 5.4 |
| No sponsor . . . . . . . . | 10 | – | – | – |

TABLE C.1.12

JOB SEEKING METHODS OF EMPLOYED HEADS OF HOUSEHOLD
(WEIGHTED PERCENTAGES)

| Source of Help | Unweighted N | Percentage Using Method* | Percentage Most Successful Method** |
|---|---|---|---|
| Through sponsor . . . . . . . . | 624 | 69.0 | 36.7 |
| Through Vietnamese friends and acquaintances . . . | 58 | 7.0 | 5.0 |
| Through American friends and acquaintances . . . . | 207 | 22.0 | 26.5 |
| Through employment agencies | 129 | 14.9 | 8.2 |
| Newspaper ads . . . . . . . | 100 | 10.9 | 6.1 |
| Telephone directory . . . . | 9 | 1.3 | 2.0 |
| Other . . . . . . . . . | 75 | 9.0 | 13.4 |

* Percentages add up to more than 100 because each person may use more than one method
** Each person was asked to indicate the one method considered to be most effective. Percentages add up to 100. Persons using only one method and successfully obtaining employment were not asked to rank the methods.

99

TABLE C.1.13

REASONS FOR NOT SEEKING EMPLOYMENT
(WEIGHTED PERCENTAGES)

| Reasons | Unweighted N | Percentage Stating Reasons ** |
|---|---|---|
| Total . . . . . . . . . . . . | 259 | |
| Attending school . . . . . . . | 82 | 35.5 |
| Keeping house . . . . . . . . | 40 | 17.3 |
| Poor health . . . . . . . . | 15 | 6.5 |
| Cannot speak English . . . . | 50 | 19.3 |
| Adequate means of support . . . | 28 | 10.8 |
| Other * . . . . . . . . . . | 44 | 17.0 |

\* "Other" includes retired, discouraged, and physically handicapped
\** Percentages add up to more than 100 because each person may give
more than one reason.

100

## TABLE C.1.14

### HOUSEHOLD INCOME BY TIME SINCE CAMP DEPARTURE
### (WEIGHTED PERCENTAGES)

| Time Since Camp Departure | Unweighted N | Under $2,500 | $2,500 to $4,999 | $5,000 to $7,499 | $7,500 to $9,999 | $10,000 and over |
|---|---|---|---|---|---|---|
| Total . . . . . . . . | 1,570 | 42.0 | 27.3 | 21.5 | 6.3 | 2.1 |
| Less than 1 month . . | 4 | 66.7 | 33.3 | - | - | - |
| 1 month or more but less than 2 months . | 94 | 38.1 | 33.8 | 20.0 | 6.9 | 1.2 |
| 2 months or more but less than 3 months . | 731 | 39.5 | 31.8 | 20.4 | 5.6 | 2.2 |
| 3 months or more . . | 740 | 44.5 | 22.5 | 23.0 | 6.9 | 2.4 |

TABLE C.1.15

TYPES OF FEDERAL ASSISTANCE BY TIME SINCE CAMP DEPARTURE
(WEIGHTED PERCENTAGES)

| Time Since Camp Departure | Unweighted N | None Received | Assistance Received | | | | | |
|---|---|---|---|---|---|---|---|---|
| | | | Food Stamps | Medical Aid | Refugee Financial Assistance | SSI | Other |
| Total . . . . . . | 1,570 | 60.4 | 21.4 | 17.9 | 18.2 | .5 | 1.6 |
| Less than 1 month | 4 | 83.3 | 16.7 | - | - | 1.1 | - |
| 1 month or more but less than 2 months . . . | 94 | 65.6 | 20.6 | 21.3 | 11.3 | 1.3 | .6 |
| 2 months or more but less than 3 months . . . | 731 | 62.5 | 22.4 | 16.0 | 13.7 | .5 | 1.3 |
| 3 months or more | 740 | 57.6 | 20.7 | 19.4 | 21.3 | .5 | 2.0 |

102

## TABLE C.1.16

## TYPES OF FEDERAL ASSISTANCE BY TYPES OF SPONSOR
### (WEIGHTED PERCENTAGES)

| VOLAG | Unweighted N | None Received | Assistance Received | | | | | |
|---|---|---|---|---|---|---|---|---|
| | | | Food Stamps | Medical Aid | Refugee Financial Assistance | SSI | Other |
| Total . . . . . . | 1,568 | 60.4 | 21.4 | 17.9 | 18.2 | .5 | 1.6 |
| Individual . . | 250 | 63.8 | 19.7 | 20.2 | 16.2 | 1.3 | .6 |
| Family . . . . . | 872 | 59.5 | 21.2 | 17.8 | 20.0 | .4 | 1.6 |
| Group . . . . . | 429 | 59.6 | 23.8 | 15.9 | 13.9 | .2 | 2.5 |
| No sponsor . . | 17 | 72.4 | 20.7 | 24.1 | 24.1 | - | 3.4 |

* Percentages add up to more than 100 because a family may receive more than one type of assistance.

TABLE C.1.17

DISTRIBUTION OF REFUGEE HOUSEHOLDS
BY CAMP

| | Number | Percentage |
|---|---|---|
| Total . . . . . . . . . . | 1,570 | |
| Pendleton . . . . . . | 556 | 35.7 |
| Chaffee . . . . . . . | 668 | 42.8 |
| Eglin . . . . . . . | 168 | 10.8 |
| Indiantown Gap . . . | 167 | 10.7 |

TABLE C.1.18

DISTRIBUTION BY REGION

|  | Number | Percentage |
|---|---|---|
| Total . . . . . . . . . | 1,570 | |
| North eastern region | 150 | 9.6 |
| Western region . . . | 514 | 32.7 |
| North central region | 305 | 19.4 |
| Southern region . . . | 561 | 35.7 |

NORTH EASTERN REGION

    Maine
    Connecticut
    New Hampshire
    Vermont
    Massachussetts
    Rhode Island
    New York
    New Jersey
    Pennsylvania

NORTH CENTRAL

    Ohio
    Indiana
    Illinois
    Michigan
    Wisconsin
    Minnesota
    Iowa
    Missouri
    North Dakota
    South Dakota
    Nebraska
    Kansas

SOUTHERN REGION

    Delaware
    Maryland
    District of Columbia
    Virginia
    West Virginia
    North Carolina
    South Carolina
    Georgia
    Florida
    Kentucky
    Tennessee
    Alabama
    Mississippi
    Arkansas
    Louisiana
    Oklahoma
    Texas

WESTERN REGION

    Montana          California
    Idaho            Alaska
    Wyoming         Hawaii
    Colorado
    New Mexico
    Arizona
    Utah
    Nevada
    Washington
    Oregon

TABLE C.1.19

DISTRIBUTION BY AGE

| | Number | Percentage |
|---|---|---|
| Total . . . . . . . . | 9,264 | |
| 0-13 . . . . . . . | 3,345 | 36.1 |
| 14-24 . . . . . . . | 2,507 | 27.1 |
| 25-34 . . . . . . . | 1,469 | 15.9 |
| 35-44 . . . . . . . | 990 | 10.7 |
| 45-54 . . . . . . . | 529 | 5.7 |
| 55-64 . . . . . . . | 253 | 2.7 |
| 65+ . . . . . . . | 126 | 1.4 |
| N/A . . . . . . . | 45 | .4 |

TABLE C.1.20

DISTRIBUTION BY FAMILY SIZE

| | Number | Percentage |
|---|---|---|
| Total . . . . . . . . . . . . | 1,570 | |
| One person family . . . . | 96 | 6.1 |
| Two person family . . . . | 137 | 8.7 |
| 3 - 5 . . . . . . . . | 533 | 33.9 |
| 6 - 8 . . . . . . . . | 508 | 32.4 |
| 9 - 11 . . . . . . . . | 196 | 12.5 |
| 12 - 14 . . . . . . . | 62 | 3.9 |
| 15 - 17 . . . . . . . | 24 | 1.5 |
| 18 and over . . . . . . | 7 | .4 |

## TABLE C.1.21

### DISTRIBUTION BY TYPES OF SPONSOR

| | Number | Percentage |
|---|---|---|
| Total . . . . . . . . . . | 1,570 | |
| Individual . . . . . . | 250 | 15.9 |
| Family . . . . . . . | 873 | 55.6 |
| Group . . . . . . | 429 | 27.3 |
| No sponsor . . . . . | 17 | 1.1 |

TABLE C.1.22

EMPLOYMENT STATUS OF HEADS OF HOUSEHOLD

| | Number | Percentage |
|---|---|---|
| Total . . . . . . . . . . | 1,570 | |
| Employed heads . . . | 895 | 57.1 |
| Unemployed heads . . . | 415 | 26.5 |
| Not in labor force . | 259 | 16.4 |

109

TABLE C.1.23

DISTRIBUTION BY FAMILY INCOME

|  | Number | Percentage |
|---|---|---|
| Total . . . . . . . . . | 1,570 | |
| Under $2,500 . . . . | 546 | 34.8 |
| $2,500 - $4,999 . . . | 479 | 30.5 |
| $5,000 - $7,499 . . . | 372 | 23.7 |
| $7,500 - $9,999 . . . | 116 | 7.4 |
| $10,000 - $12,499 . . | 26 | 1.7 |
| $12,500 - $14,999 . . | 5 | .3 |
| $15,000 - $19,999 . . | 9 | .6 |
| $20,000 - $24,999 . . | 2 | .1 |
| $25,000 - $29,999 . . | 1 | .1 |
| $30,000 and above . . | - | - |

TABLE C.1.24

DISTRIBUTION BY PLACE OF RESIDENCE

| | Number | Percentage |
|---|---|---|
| Total . . . . . . . . . . . | 1,570 | |
| Separate residence . . | 827 | 52.7 |
| Sponsor's home . . . . | 626 | 39.9 |
| Friend's home . . . . . | 33 | 2.1 |
| Relative's home . . . . | 43 | 2.7 |
| Other . . . . . . . . | 39 | 2.5 |

TABLE C.2.1

EMPLOYMENT STATUS OF PERSONS 16 YEARS AND OLDER BY AGE AND SEX

| Age | MALE | | | | FEMALE | | | |
|-----|------|---|---|---|--------|---|---|---|
| | N | % | Employed | Unemployed | N | % | Employed | Unemployed |
| Total . . . . . | 1988 | 100 | 82.0 | 18.0 | 789 | 100 | 70.1 | 29.9 |
| 16 - 24 . . | 743 | 100 | 82.4 | 17.6 | 310 | 100 | 72.6 | 27.4 |
| 25 - 34 . . | 687 | 100 | 82.7 | 17.3 | 295 | 100 | 70.8 | 29.2 |
| 35 - 44 . . | 347 | 100 | 82.7 | 17.3 | 123 | 100 | 65.8 | 34.5 |
| 45 - 54 . . | 166 | 100 | 84.9 | 15.1 | 53 | 100 | 62.3 | 37.7 |
| 55+ . . | 45 | 100 | 51.1 | 48.9 | 8 | 100 | 62.5 | 37.5 |

TABLE C.2.2

REASONS FOR JOB DISSATISFACTION BY SEX AND DEGREE
OF DISSATISFACTION

| Degree of Dissatisfaction | N | Work Too Demand- ing | Low Sala- ry | Irreg- ular Sche- dule | Not In Line With Train- ing | Tempo- rary Job | No Possi- bility For Advan- cement | Other |
|---|---|---|---|---|---|---|---|---|
| Total . . . . . . . . | 1310 | 26.4 | 37.2 | 11.6 | 63.1 | 46.0 | 47.0 | 5.0 |
| Somewhat satisfied . . | 1027 | 22.6 | 35.4 | 10.7 | 60.1 | 45.8 | 46.2 | 4.3 |
| Not satisfied  . . . | 283 | 40.6 | 43.8 | 15.2 | 74.2 | 46.6 | 50.2 | 7.8 |
| Male  . . . . . . . | 1026 | 28.2 | 36.8 | 11.5 | 66.5 | 46.2 | 48.7 | 5.2 |
| Somewhat satisfied . . | 795 | 24.2 | 35.0 | 10.6 | 63.3 | 46.0 | 48.1 | 4.8 |
| Not satisfied . . . . | 231 | 42.0 | 43.3 | 14.7 | 77.5 | 46.8 | 51.1 | 6.9 |
| Female  . . . . . . | 284 | 20.4 | 38.7 | 12.3 | 51.0 | 45.1 | 40.8 | 4.2 |
| Somewhat satisfied . . | 232 | 17.2 | 37.1 | 11.2 | 49.1 | 44.8 | 39.7 | 2.6 |
| Not satisfied. . . . | 52 | 34.6 | 46.2 | 17.3 | 59.6 | 46.2 | 46.2 | 11.5 |

*Percentages add up to more than 100 because a person may have more than one reason

113

## TABLE C.2.3

EMPLOYMENT STATUS OF PERSONS 16 YEARS AND OLDER BY SEX AND
RELATIONSHIP TO HEADS OF HOUSEHOLD

| Relationship to Household Head | MALE | | | | FEMALE | | | |
|---|---|---|---|---|---|---|---|---|
| | N | % | Employed | Unemployed | N | % | Employed | Unemployed |
| Total . . . . . . | 1988 | 100 | 82.0 | 18.0 | 789 | 100 | 70.1 | 29.9 |
| Head . . . . . . | 1119 | 100 | 82.9 | 17.1 | 121 | 100 | 80.2 | 19.8 |
| Spouse . . . . . | 16 | 100 | 68.7 | 31.3 | 264 | 100 | 64.8 | 35.2 |
| Child or spouse | 198 | 100 | 78.8 | 21.2 | 190 | 100 | 72.1 | 27.9 |
| Grandchild/ nephew/niece . | 44 | 100 | 81.8 | 18.2 | 10 | 100 | 70.0 | 30.0 |
| Parent or spouse . . . . | 15 | 100 | 60.0 | 40.0 | 11 | 100 | 72.8 | 27.2 |
| Other relative. | 284 | 100 | 77.1 | 22.9 | 174 | 100 | 68.4 | 31.6 |
| Unrelated/ no answer . . . . | 312 | 100 | 87.2 | 12.8 | 19 | 100 | 73.7 | 26.3 |

114

**TABLE C.2.4**

**EMPLOYMENT STATUS OF HEADS OF HOUSEHOLD
BY VIETNAM OCCUPATION**

| Vietnam Occupation | Total N | Total % | Employed | Unemployed |
|---|---|---|---|---|
| Total . . . . . . . . | 1241 | 100 | 82.7 | 17.3 |
| White Collar . . . . | 837 | 100 | 82.3 | 17.7 |
| Professional . . . | 272 | 100 | 84.9 | 15.1 |
| Managers . . . . | 369 | 100 | 82.1 | 17.9 |
| Clerical and Sales. | 196 | 100 | 79.1 | 20.9 |
| Blue Collar . . . . . | 336 | 100 | 83.9 | 16.1 |
| Craftsman . . . . . | 112 | 100 | 83.9 | 16.1 |
| Operatives and Transport . . . | 48 | 100 | 91.7 | 8.3 |
| Laborers . . . . . | 149 | 100 | 82.6 | 17.4 |
| Other Blue Collar . | 27 | 100 | 77.8 | 22.2 |
| Not Ascertained . . . | 68 | 100 | 80.9 | 19.1 |

**TABLE C.2.5**

PRESENT OCCUPATION OF HEADS OF HOUSEHOLD BY VIETNAM OCCUPATION

| Vietnam Occupation | Total N | % | Present Occupation | | | | | | |
|---|---|---|---|---|---|---|---|---|---|
| | | | White Collar | | | Blue Collar | | | |
| | | | Profes-sional | Mana-gers | Clerical and Sales | Crafts-man | Operatives Transport | Laborers | Other Blue Collar |
| Total . . . . . . | 1026 | 100 | 6.6 | 1.0 | 13.2 | 21.9 | 6.2 | 16.7 | 34.4 |
| White Collar . . . . | 689 | 100 | 8.7 | 1.5 | 17.0 | 17.6 | 7.8 | 16.7 | 30.8 |
| Professional . . . | 231 | 100 | 16.0 | 1.7 | 17.7 | 17.3 | 6.5 | 13.9 | 26.8 |
| Managers . . . | 303 | 100 | 5.9 | 1.7 | 12.9 | 19.1 | 10.6 | 18.8 | 31.0 |
| Clerical and Sales. | 155 | 100 | 3.2 | .6 | 23.9 | 14.8 | 4.5 | 16.8 | 36.1 |
| Blue Collar . . . . | 282 | 100 | 2.1 | – | 4.3 | 32.6 | 3.5 | 16.7 | 40.8 |
| Craftsman. . . . | 94 | 100 | 5.3 | – | 3.2 | 46.8 | 2.1 | 17.0 | 25.5 |
| Operatives and Transport . . . | 44 | 100 | – | – | 6.8 | 25.0 | 4.5 | 9.1 | 54.5 |
| Laborers . . . | 123 | 100 | – | – | 4.1 | 26.0 | 4.1 | 20.3 | 45.5 |
| Other Blue Collar . | 21 | 100 | 4.8 | – | 4.8 | 23.8 | 4.8 | 9.5 | 52.4 |
| Not Ascertained . . | 55 | 100 | 3.6 | – | 10.9 | 21.8 | – | 16.4 | 47.3 |

## TABLE C.2.6

### CHILDREN ENROLLED IN SCHOOL BY TYPE OF SCHOOL AND AGE AND SEX

| Age and Sex | Total N | Total % | Not Attending School | Day Care Or Nursery School | Elementary School | Secondary School | Other |
|---|---|---|---|---|---|---|---|
| Total | 3302 | 100 | 19.5 | 9.2 | 34.7 | 29.0 | 7.4 |
| 3 – 4 | 442 | 100 | 81.0 | 18.6 | - | - | .5 |
| 5 – 8 | 811 | 100 | 10.0 | 27.1 | 61.7 | - | .5 |
| 9 – 12 | 759 | 100 | 3.8 | .4 | 77.5 | 17.5 | .5 |
| 13 – 16 | 688 | 100 | 4.1 | - | 8.1 | 84.6 | 2.8 |
| 17 – 19 | 602 | 100 | 24.4 | - | - | 39.4 | 35.7 |
| Male | 1770 | 100 | 18.6 | 9.7 | 33.8 | 29.1 | 8.6 |
| 3 – 4 | 230 | 100 | 77.0 | 22.6 | - | - | .4 |
| 5 – 8 | 430 | 100 | 10.5 | 27.2 | 60.7 | - | .7 |
| 9 – 12 | 401 | 100 | 3.5 | .7 | 76.6 | 18.5 | .7 |
| 13 – 16 | 375 | 100 | 3.5 | - | 7.5 | 85.3 | 3.2 |
| 17 – 19 | 334 | 100 | 24.0 | - | - | 35.0 | 40.1 |
| Female | 1532 | 100 | 20.5 | 8.7 | 35.8 | 28.9 | 5.9 |
| 3 – 4 | 212 | 100 | 85.4 | 14.2 | - | - | .5 |
| 5 – 8 | 381 | 100 | 9.4 | 27.0 | 62.7 | - | .3 |
| 9 – 12 | 358 | 100 | 4.2 | - | 78.5 | 16.5 | .3 |
| 13 – 16 | 313 | 100 | 4.8 | - | 8.9 | 83.7 | 2.2 |
| 17 – 19 | 268 | 100 | 25.8 | - | - | 44.8 | 30.2 |

## TABLE C.2.7

### CHILDREN REPEATING GRADE COMPLETED IN VIETNAM
### BY AGE AND SEX

| Age and Sex | Total N | Total % | Repeating Grade or Year | Not Repeating Grade or Year |
|---|---|---|---|---|
| Total | 2083 | 100 | 49.2 | 50.8 |
| 5 - 8 . . . . . . . . | 498 | 100 | 50.6 | 49.4 |
| 9 - 12 . . . . . . . | 713 | 100 | 53.6 | 46.4 |
| 13 - 16 . . . . . . . | 635 | 100 | 44.1 | 55.9 |
| 17 - 19 . . . . . . | 237 | 100 | 46.8 | 53.2 |
| Male | 1103 | 100 | 51.6 | 48.4 |
| 5 - 8 . . . . . . . . | 260 | 100 | 56.1 | 43.8 |
| 9 - 12 . . . . . . . | 378 | 100 | 57.1 | 42.9 |
| 13 - 16 . . . . . . . | 346 | 100 | 43.6 | 56.4 |
| 17 - 19 . . . . . . | 119 | 100 | 47.1 | 52.9 |
| Female | 980 | 100 | 46.5 | 53.5 |
| 5 - 8 . . . . . . . . | 238 | 100 | 44.5 | 55.5 |
| 9 - 12 . . . . . . . | 335 | 100 | 49.6 | 50.4 |
| 13 - 16 . . . . . . . | 289 | 100 | 44.6 | 55.4 |
| 17 - 19 . . . . . . | 118 | 100 | 46.6 | 53.4 |

118

**TABLE C.2.8**

REASONS STATED BY SCHOOL FOR REPEATING GRADE
BY AGE AND SEX

| Age and Sex | N | English Difficulty | Vietnamese Course Content Not Comparable | Child's Ability | Child's Age | Other |
|---|---|---|---|---|---|---|
| Total | 1025 | 84.1 | 15.7 | 6.2 | 5.6 | 9.0 |
| 5 - 8 | 252 | 82.9 | 13.5 | 8.0 | 6.0 | 10.3 |
| 9 - 12 | 382 | 86.4 | 16.5 | 5.2 | 5.2 | 7.6 |
| 13 - 16 | 280 | 82.5 | 15.3 | 5.4 | 6.8 | 9.3 |
| 17 - 19 | 111 | 82.9 | 18.9 | 8.1 | 2.7 | 9.9 |
| Male | 569 | 84.9 | 17.0 | 7.2 | 5.4 | 9.1 |
| 5 - 8 | 146 | 82.9 | 18.1 | 10.3 | 6.8 | 11.0 |
| 9 - 12 | 216 | 84.3 | 16.2 | 5.1 | 7.1 | 8.8 |
| 13 - 16 | 151 | 86.7 | 19.2 | 6.0 | 5.3 | 8.6 |
| 17 - 19 | 56 | 87.5 | 19.6 | 10.7 | - | 7.1 |
| Female | 456 | 83.1 | 14.0 | 5.0 | 5.7 | 8.8 |
| 5 - 8 | 106 | 83.0 | 11.3 | 4.7 | 4.7 | 9.4 |
| 9 - 12 | 166 | 89.1 | 16.9 | 5.4 | 4.2 | 6.0 |
| 13 - 16 | 129 | 77.5 | 10.8 | 4.6 | 8.5 | 10.1 |
| 17 - 19 | 55 | 78.2 | 18.2 | 5.4 | 5.4 | 12.7 |

*Percentages add up to more than 100 because there may be more than one reason for each student.

119

## TABLE C.2.9

### MONTHLY WAGES AND SALARY INCOME OF HOUSEHOLDS BY TIME SINCE CAMP DEPARTURE

| Time Since Camp Departure | Total | | Monthly Wages and Salary Income | | | | | |
|---|---|---|---|---|---|---|---|---|
| | N | % | Zero Wages | Under $200 | $200-399 | $400-599 | $600-799 | $800 and over |
| Total . . . . . . . . | 1424 | 100 | 19.9 | 3.6 | 15.0 | 19.2 | 12.5 | 29.7 |
| Less than 2 months | 14 | 100 | 28.6 | 7.1 | 7.1 | 14.3 | 14.3 | 28.6 |
| 2 months, less than 3 | 233 | 100 | 24.5 | 3.4 | 17.6 | 14.2 | 13.7 | 26.6 |
| 3 months, less than 4 | 361 | 100 | 17.7 | 3.9 | 13.9 | 20.8 | 14.1 | 29.6 |
| 4 months, less than 5 | 352 | 100 | 15.6 | 2.0 | 15.1 | 22.2 | 11.9 | 33.2 |
| 5 months, less than 6 | 241 | 100 | 20.3 | 5.4 | 14.9 | 17.0 | 12.4 | 29.9 |
| 6 months or more . . | 223 | 100 | 24.7 | 3.6 | 14.8 | 20.2 | 9.4 | 27.4 |

**TABLE C.2.10**

MONTHLY HOUSEHOLD INCOME BY COMPONENTS OF INCOME

| Household Income | N | Wages and Salary Income | Government Transfer Payments | Other Financial Contributions |
|---|---|---|---|---|
| Total . . . . . . | 1424 | 80.6 | 13.6 | 6.1 |
| Under $200 . . | 250 | 18.8 | 14.4 | 6.2 |
| $200 to $399 . . | 220 | 81.4 | 15.0 | 8.6 |
| $400 to $599 . . | 298 | 91.6 | 16.8 | 6.0 |
| $600 to $799 . . | 194 | 96.9 | 12.9 | 5.2 |
| $800 or more . . | 462 | 99.8 | 10.8 | 5.4 |

*Percentages add up to more than 100 because the income of a household may be made up of more than one component.

**TABLE C.2.11**

TYPES OF FEDERAL ASSISTANCE BY TIME
SINCE DEPARTURE FROM CAMP

| Length of Time Since Camp Departure | N | None Received | Food Stamps | Assistance Received * Medical Aid | Refugee Financial Assistance | SSI |
|---|---|---|---|---|---|---|
| Total . . . . . . . . | 1424 | 58.0 | 25.6 | 23.7 | 13.4 | 2.8 |
| Less than 2 months . | 14 | 42.9 | 35.7 | 28.6 | 21.4 | .9 |
| 2 months, less than 3 | 233 | 63.1 | 24.0 | 16.3 | 10.3 | 2.8 |
| 3 months, less than 4 | 361 | 61.2 | 25.2 | 19.9 | 12.5 | 4.0 |
| 4 months, less than 5 | 352 | 55.1 | 25.6 | 24.7 | 12.8 | 1.7 |
| 5 months, less than 6 | 241 | 58.5 | 25.7 | 27.0 | 11.6 | 4.5 |
| 6 months or more . . | 223 | 52.5 | 27.4 | 31.8 | 20.6 | |

* Percentages add up to more than 100 because a family may receive more than one type of assistance.

TABLE C.2.12

MONTHLY HOUSING COSTS BY RESIDENCE ARRANGEMENT

| Residence Arrangement | Total N | Total % | No Payment | Less Than 100 | 101 to 150 | 151 to 200 | 201 to 250 | 251 to 300 | 301 to 350 | 351 or More |
|---|---|---|---|---|---|---|---|---|---|---|
| Total . . . . . . . | 1125 | 100 | 39.3 | 13.4 | 14.7 | 18.3 | 7.9 | 3.3 | 1.6 | .1 |
| Separate residence | 785 | 100 | 19.7 | 15.6 | 20.9 | 25.5 | 11.2 | 3.6 | 2.2 | 1.1 |
| Own . . . . . . . | 26 | 100 | – | 30.8 | 30.8 | 11.5 | 15.4 | 3.8 | 3.8 | – |
| Rent . . . . . . . | 675 | 100 | 10.5 | 16.7 | 23.1 | 29.3 | 12.4 | 4.0 | 2.4 | 1.3 |
| Lent by friend . | 84 | 100 | 96.4 | 2.4 | 1.2 | – | – | – | – | – |
| Sponsor's house . | 286 | 100 | 87.8 | 8.0 | 1.7 | 1.4 | – | .3 | – | .3 |
| Friend's house. . | 13 | 100 | 61.5 | 38.5 | – | – | – | – | – | – |
| Relative's house . | 8 | 100 | 75.0 | 25.0 | – | – | – | – | – | – |
| Other . . . . . . | 33 | 100 | 72.7 | 18.2 | 6.1 | – | 3.0 | – | – | – |

## TABLE C.2.13

### OCCUPATIONAL LEVEL OF EMPLOYED -HEADS
### BETWEEN SURVEY I AND SURVEY II

| Type of Occupation | Survey I N | Survey I % | Survey II N | Survey II % |
|---|---|---|---|---|
| Total . . . . . . . . . . . . . | 234 | 100 | 301 | 100 |
| White Collar . . . . . . . . | | | | |
| Professional . . . . . . . | 11 | 4.7 | 33 | 11.0 |
| Managerial . . . . . | 3 | 1.3 | 6 | 2.0 |
| Clerical and Sales . . . | 43 | 18.4 | 54 | 17.9 |
| Blue Collar . . . . . . . | | | | |
| Craftsman . . . . . . . | 48 | 20.5 | 49 | 16.3 |
| Operatives and Transport . | 5 | 2.1 | 19 | 6.3 |
| Laborers . . . . . . . | 31 | 13.2 | 43 | 14.3 |
| Other . . . . . . . . | 87 | 37.2 | 97 | 32.2 |
| Not ascertained . . . . . . | 6 | 2.6 | - | - |

**TABLE C.2.14**

MONTHLY WAGES AND SALARY INCOME OF EMPLOYED PERSONS
16 YEARS AND OLDER BETWEEN SURVEY I AND SURVEY II

| Wages and Salary Income | Survey I | Survey II |
|---|---|---|
| Total . . . . . . . . . . . . . . | 454 | 618 |
| Head . . . . . . . . . | 234 | 301 |
| Zero income . . . . | – | 1.0 |
| Less than $200 . . . | 2.6% | 6.3% |
| $200 – $399 . . . | 35.0% | 29.5% |
| $400 – $599 . . . | 40.2% | 37.2% |
| $600 – $799 . . . | 13.7% | 16.0% |
| $800 – over . . . | 5.1% | 10.0% |
| Not ascertained . . . | 3.4% | – |
| Other . . . . . . . . | 220 | 317 |
| Zero income . . . . | 11.4% | 2.5% |
| Less than $200 . . . | – | 14.2% |
| $200 – $399 . . . | 59.5% | 43.5% |
| $400 – $599 . . . | 24.1% | 31.2% |
| $600 – $799 . . . | 2.3% | 6.6% |
| $800 – over . . . | 0.9% | 1.9% |
| Not ascertained . . . | 1.8% | – |

## TABLE C.2.15

### FEDERAL ASSISTANCE RECEIVED BY REFUGEE HOUSEHOLDS
### BETWEEN SURVEY I AND SURVEY II

| Type of Federal Assistance | Survey I | Survey II |
|---|---|---|
| Total . . . . . . . . . . . . . . . | <u>446</u> | <u>446</u> |
| Percentages Receiving . . . . . . . . | | |
| Food stamps . . . . . . . . . . | 26.0% | 27.6% |
| Medical aid . . . . . . . . . . | 19.7% | 30.5% |
| Refugee financial assistance. . . . | 19.1% | 17.3% |
| SSI . . . . . . . . . . . . . . | .4% | 3.1% |

126

**TABLE C.2.16**

LABOR FORCE PARTICIPATION OF VIETNAM REFUGEES IN SURVEY I AND SURVEY II
BY PROFICIENCY IN ENGLISH

| Proficiency In English | Survey I | | | | Survey II (Cross-Sectional*) | | | |
| | Persons 14 years and older | | | | Persons 16 years and older | | | |
| | N | % | In Labor Force | Not In Labor Force | N | % | In Labor Force | Not In Labor Force |
|---|---|---|---|---|---|---|---|---|
| Total | 5,879 | 100 | 54.4 | 45.6 | 3,128 | 100 | 64.0 | 36.0 |
| **Understand English** | | | | | | | | |
| Not at all | 636 | 100 | 20.4 | 79.6 | 441 | 100 | 35.1 | 64.9 |
| Some | 3,784 | 100 | 52.2 | 47.8 | 2,192 | 100 | 67.6 | 32.4 |
| Well | 1,300 | 100 | 77.0 | 23.0 | 446 | 100 | 81.4 | 18.6 |
| **Speak English** | | | | | | | | |
| Not at all | 669 | 100 | 21.7 | 78.3 | 453 | 100 | 35.5 | 64.5 |
| Some | 3,782 | 100 | 52.6 | 47.4 | 2,191 | 100 | 67.7 | 32.3 |
| Well | 1,272 | 100 | 76.7 | 23.3 | 437 | 100 | 81.2 | 18.8 |
| **Read English** | | | | | | | | |
| Not at all | 687 | 100 | 21.1 | 78.9 | 469 | 100 | 36.9 | 63.1 |
| Some | 3,671 | 100 | 51.8 | 48.2 | 2,131 | 100 | 67.2 | 32.8 |
| Well | 1,385 | 100 | 77.2 | 22.8 | 478 | 100 | 82.2 | 17.8 |
| **Write English** | | | | | | | | |
| Not at all | 717 | 100 | 22.3 | 77.7 | 477 | 100 | 37.5 | 62.5 |
| Some | 3,682 | 100 | 52.3 | 47.7 | 2,142 | 100 | 67.4 | 32.6 |
| Well | 1,321 | 100 | 76.8 | 23.2 | 460 | 100 | 81.7 | 18.3 |

*The Cross-Sectional sample includes only people who left camp after July 15, 1975.

**TABLE C.2.17**

COMPARISON OF DEGREE OF EDUCATIONAL ATTAINMENT FOR LABOR FORCE
PARTICIPANTS IN SURVEY I AND SURVEY II BY SEX

| Educational Attainment | Male | | | | Female | | | |
|---|---|---|---|---|---|---|---|---|
| | Survey I | | Survey II * | | Survey I | | Survey II* | |
| | N | % | N | % | N | % | N | % |
| Total | 1,989 | 100.0 | 1,499 | 100.0 | 1,181 | 100.0 | 504 | 100.0 |
| None . . . . . . | 103 | 5.2 | 201 | 13.4 | 137 | 11.6 | 142 | 28.2 |
| Primary Diploma | 85 | 4.3 | 149 | 10.0 | 99 | 8.4 | 46 | 9.1 |
| BEPSI/DEPSI/BE . | 317 | 15.9 | 260 | 17.3 | 294 | 24.9 | 72 | 14.3 |
| BACC I . . . . . | 188 | 9.4 | 159 | 10.6 | 129 | 10.9 | 57 | 11.3 |
| BACC II . . . . | 684 | 34.4 | 554 | 37.0 | 326 | 27.6 | 148 | 29.4 |
| University . . . | 487 | 24.5 | 144 | 9.6 | 152 | 12.9 | 34 | 6.7 |
| Other . . . . . | 49 | 2.5 | 32 | 2.1 | 9 | .7 | 5 | 1.0 |
| Not ascertained | 76 | 3.8 | - | - | 35 | 3.0 | - | - |

*Survey II data are based on the cross-section sample only.  This
sample includes people who left camp after July 15, 1975.

128

**TABLE C.2.18**

EMPLOYMENT STATUS OF VIETNAM REFUGEES IN SURVEY I AND SURVEY II
BY SEX AND EDUCATIONAL ATTAINMENT

| Educational Attainment | Survey I | | | Survey II (Cross-sectional only)* | | |
|---|---|---|---|---|---|---|
| | Persons 14 years and older | | | Persons 16 years and older | | |
| | N | Employed | Unemployed | N | Employed | Unemployed |
| **MALES** | | | | | | |
| Total | 1989 | 100 | 69.2 | 31.8 | 1499 | 100 | 81.8 | 18.2 |
| None | 103 | 100 | 56.0 | 44.0 | 201 | 100 | 86.1 | 13.9 |
| Primary Diploma | 85 | 100 | 72.0 | 28.0 | 149 | 100 | 76.5 | 23.5 |
| BEPSI/DEPSI/BE | 317 | 100 | 68.0 | 32.0 | 260 | 100 | 80.4 | 19.6 |
| BACC I | 188 | 100 | 65.0 | 35.0 | 159 | 100 | 86.2 | 13.8 |
| BACC II | 684 | 100 | 73.0 | 27.0 | 554 | 100 | 82.5 | 17.5 |
| University | 487 | 100 | 64.0 | 36.0 | 144 | 100 | 75.0 | 25.0 |
| Other | 49 | 100 | 53.0 | 47.0 | 32 | 100 | 87.5 | 12.5 |
| **FEMALES** | | | | | | |
| Total | 1181 | 100 | 50.9 | 49.1 | 504 | 100 | 68.3 | 31.7 |
| None | 137 | 100 | 37.0 | 63.0 | 142 | 100 | 67.6 | 32.4 |
| Primary Diploma | 99 | 100 | 55.0 | 45.0 | 46 | 100 | 56.5 | 43.5 |
| BEPSI/DEPSI/BE | 294 | 100 | 55.0 | 45.0 | 72 | 100 | 62.5 | 37.5 |
| BACC I | 129 | 100 | 51.0 | 49.0 | 57 | 100 | 73.7 | 26.3 |
| BACC II | 326 | 100 | 51.0 | 49.0 | 146 | 100 | 70.9 | 29.1 |
| University | 152 | 100 | 53.0 | 47.0 | 34 | 100 | 76.5 | 23.5 |
| Other | 9 | 100 | - | - | 5 | 100 | - | - |

*The cross-sectional sample includes only people who left camp after July 15, 1975.

129

**TABLE C.2.19**

EMPLOYMENT OF HOUSEHOLD HEADS AT TIME OF SURVEY I AND SURVEY II
BY TYPE OF OCCUPATION

| Occupation | Survey I | | Survey II (Cross-Sectional only)* | |
|---|---|---|---|---|
| | N | % | N | % |
| Total | 897 | 100.0 | 725 | 100.0 |
| **White-Collar** | | | | |
| Professional . . . | 64 | 7.1 | 35 | 4.8 |
| Managerial . . . | 13 | 1.4 | 4 | .6 |
| Clerical and Sales | 175 | 19.5 | 81 | 11.2 |
| **Blue-Collar** | | | | |
| Craftsman . . . | 146 | 16.3 | 176 | 24.3 |
| Operatives and Transport . . . | 24 | 2.7 | 45 | 6.2 |
| Laborers . . . . | 108 | 12.1 | 128 | 17.6 |
| Other . . . . . | 307 | 34.2 | 256 | 35.3 |
| Not ascertained | 60 | 6.7 | – | – |

*The cross-sectional sample includes only people who left camp
after July 15, 1975.

130

**TABLE C.2.20**

DISTRIBUTION OF REFUGEE HOUSEHOLDS
BY REGION

| Region | N | % |
|---|---|---|
| Total | 1424 | 100.0 |
| North eastern Region . . . | 251 | 17.6 |
| Western Region . . . | 411 | 28.9 |
| North central Region . . . | 347 | 24.4 |
| Southern Region . . . | 415 | 29.1 |

131

**TABLE C.2.21**

DISTRIBUTION OF REFUGEES BY AGE

| Age | N | % |
|---|---|---|
| Total | 7498 | 100.0 |
| 0 – 4 . . . . . | 908 | 12.1 |
| 5 – 14 . . . . | 1910 | 25.5 |
| 15 – 24 . . . . | 1977 | 26.4 |
| 25 – 34 . . . . | 1340 | 17.9 |
| 35 – 44 . . . . | 696 | 9.3 |
| 45 – 54 . . . . | 363 | 4.8 |
| 55 – 64 . . . . | 202 | 2.7 |
| 65 and over . . . . | 102 | 1.4 |

TABLE C.2.22

DISTRIBUTION OF REFUGEES BY AGE AND SEX

| Age and Sex | N | % |
|---|---|---|
| Total | 7498 | 100.0 |
| Male | 4110 | 54.8 |
| 0 - 4 . . . . . . . | 468 | 6.2 |
| 5 - 14 . . . . . | 1019 | 13.6 |
| 15 - 24 . . . . . | 1157 | 15.4 |
| 25 - 34 . . . . . | 775 | 10.3 |
| 35 - 44 . . . . . | 389 | 5.2 |
| 45 - 54 . . . . . | 191 | 2.5 |
| 55 - 64 . . . . . | 80 | 1.1 |
| 65 and over . . . | 31 | .4 |
| Female | 3388 | 45.2 |
| 0 - 4 . . . . . . . | 440 | 5.9 |
| 5 - 14 . . . . . | 891 | 11.9 |
| 15 - 24 . . . . . | 820 | 10.9 |
| 25 - 34 . . . . . | 565 | 7.5 |
| 35 - 44 . . . . . | 307 | 4.1 |
| 45 - 54 . . . . . | 172 | 2.3 |
| 55 - 64 . . . . . | 122 | 1.6 |
| 65 and over . . . | 71 | .9 |

TABLE C.2.23

PERCENTAGE OF PERSONS ENROLLED IN SCHOOL BY
AGE, SEX, AND LEVEL OF SCHOOL

| Age | Male | | | | | | | Female | | | | | | |
|---|---|---|---|---|---|---|---|---|---|---|---|---|---|---|
| | Total | Not En-roll-ed | Pre-pri-mary | Ele-men-tary | High Sch. | Col-lege | Other | Total | Not En-roll-ed | Pre-pri-mary | Ele-men-tary | High Sch. | Col-lege | Other |
| 3 – 5 . . . . . | 347 | 58.8 | 37.2 | 3.7 | | | .3 | 308 | 70.0 | 28.0 | 2.0 | | | |
| 6 – 11 . . . | 613 | 5.6 | 7.0 | 82.5 | 4.9 | | | 560 | 13.5 | 5.9 | 77.2 | 3.4 | | |
| 12 – 18 . . | 686 | 15.7 | | 11.5 | 69.1 | 1.3 | 2.4 | 582 | 28.4 | | 9.9 | 59.2 | .6 | 1.9 |
| 19 – 25 . . | 902 | 82.5 | | | 1.9 | 4.1 | 11.5 | 557 | 88.6 | | .1 | 2.3 | 1.9 | 7.1 |
| 26 – 34 . . | 633 | 88.2 | .1 | | | 1.8 | 10.0 | 481 | 93.4 | .2 | .3 | .2 | .5 | 5.4 |
| 35 and over . | 691 | 93.2 | .1 | .1 | .1 | .2 | 6.3 | 672 | 95.1 | .1 | | .3 | .2 | 4.3 |

TABLE C.2.24

LENGTH OF TIME FEDERAL ASSISTANCE HAS BEEN
RECEIVED BY TYPE OF FEDERAL ASSISTANCE

| Type of Federal Assistance | Total | | Less than 1 month | 1 month - less than 2 months | 2 months - less than 3 months | 3 months - less than 4 months | 4 months or more |
|---|---|---|---|---|---|---|---|
| | N | % | | | | | |
| Food Stamps . . . . . | 360 | 100 | 6.2 | 20.2 | 31.7 | 21.1 | 20.8 |
| Refugee Financial Assistance . . . . . | 188 | 100 | 3.7 | 20.2 | 30.3 | 25.5 | 20.2 |
| SSI . . . . . . . . | 44 | 100 | - | 13.6 | 20.5 | 38.6 | 27.3 |

135

TABLE C.3.1

LABOR FORCE PARTICIPATION OF PERSONS 16 YEARS AND OLDER BY SEX
AND LENGTH OF TIME SINCE DEPARTURE FROM CAMP

| Sex and Length of Time Since Camp Departure | Total | | In Labor Force | | Not in Labor Force |
|---|---|---|---|---|---|
| | N | % | Employed | Unemployed | |
| Total . . . . . . . . . | 1714 | 100 | 55.7 | 7.9 | 35.7 |
| 6 months, less than 7 . . . | 20 | 100 | 40.0 | 45.0 | 15.0 |
| 7 months, less than 8 . . . | 127 | 100 | 54.3 | 8.7 | 36.2 |
| 8 months, less than 9 . . . | 150 | 100 | 55.3 | 9.3 | 35.3 |
| 9 months, less than 10 . . . | 251 | 100 | 50.6 | 9.6 | 39.8 |
| 10 months or more . . . | 1166 | 100 | 57.3 | 6.7 | 35.2 |
| Male . . . . . . . . . | 955 | 100 | 71.9 | 8.1 | 19.7 |
| 6 months, less than 7 . . . | 14 | 100 | 50.0 | 35.7 | 14.3 |
| 7 months, less than 8 . . . | 75 | 100 | 72.0 | 8.0 | 20.0 |
| 8 months, less than 9 . . . | 84 | 100 | 70.2 | 11.9 | 17.9 |
| 9 months, less than 10 . . . | 135 | 100 | 65.2 | 11.9 | 23.0 |
| 10 months or more . . . | 647 | 100 | 74.0 | 6.2 | 19.3 |
| Female . . . . . . . . . | 759 | 100 | 35.3 | 7.8 | 55.9 |
| 6 months, less than 7 . . . | 6 | 100 | 16.7 | 66.7 | 16.7 |
| 7 months, less than 8 . . . | 52 | 100 | 28.8 | 9.6 | 59.6 |
| 8 months, less than 9 . . . | 66 | 100 | 36.4 | 6.1 | 57.6 |
| 9 months, less than 10 . . . | 116 | 100 | 33.6 | 6.9 | 59.5 |
| 10 months or more . . . | 519 | 100 | 36.4 | 7.3 | 54.9 |

## TABLE C.3.2

### LABOR FORCE PARTICIPATION OF PERSONS 16 YEARS AND OLDER BY SEX AND RELATIONSHIP TO HEADS OF HOUSEHOLD

| Relationship To Household Head | MALES * | | | | | | FEMALES * | | | | | |
|---|---|---|---|---|---|---|---|---|---|---|---|---|
| | Total | | In Labor Force | | Not in Labor Force | | Total | | In Labor Force | | Not in Labor Force | |
| | N | % | Em-ployed | Unem-ployed | | | N | % | Em-ployed | Unem-ployed | | |
| Total . . . . . . | 955 | 100 | 71.9 | 8.1 | 19.7 | | 759 | 100 | 35.3 | 7.8 | 55.9 | |
| Head . . . . . . | 546 | 100 | 81.1 | 8.4 | 10.3 | | 71 | 100 | 60.6 | 5.6 | 32.4 | |
| Spouse. . . . . | 5 | 100 | 100.0 | | | | 345 | 100 | 29.6 | 8.4 | 61.4 | |
| Child or spouse . | 183 | 100 | 52.5 | 6.0 | 41.0 | | 169 | 100 | 37.3 | 5.9 | 53.8 | |
| Grandchild/ nephew/niece . . | 13 | 100 | 61.5 | 7.7 | 23.1 | | 12 | 100 | 50.0 | 25.0 | 25.0 | |
| Parent or spouse. | 23 | 100 | 34.8 | 8.7 | 56.5 | | 69 | 100 | 4.3 | 5.8 | 89.9 | |
| Other relative. . | 106 | 100 | 56.6 | 11.3 | 32.1 | | 91 | 100 | 54.9 | 9.9 | 35.2 | |
| Unrelated/no answer . . . . | 79 | 100 | 84.8 | 6.3 | 8.9 | | 2 | 100 | 50.0 | | 50.0 | |

* Missing cases are not presented in this table. Therefore percentages in some rows add up to less than 100.0%.

137

TABLE C.3.3

REASONS FOR NOT SEEKING EMPLOYMENT BY AGE AND SEX

| Age and Sex | Total N | Total % | Reasons Given* Attending School | Keeping House | Poor Health | Can Not Speak English | Other Means of Support | Dis-couraged | Other |
|---|---|---|---|---|---|---|---|---|---|
| Total | 612 | 100 | 49.2 | 36.6 | 13.2 | 11.3 | 2.5 | .3 | 3.1 |
| 16 - 19 . . . | 172 | 100 | 94.8 | 5.8 | .6 | .6 | | | 3.5 |
| 20 - 24 . . . | 85 | 100 | 56.5 | 35.3 | 4.7 | 4.7 | 2.4 | .8 | 5.0 |
| 25 - 34 . . . | 119 | 100 | 37.8 | 60.5 | 5.9 | 14.3 | .8 | | 1.4 |
| 35 - 44 . . . | 70 | 100 | 34.3 | 61.4 | 7.1 | 15.7 | | | |
| 45 - 54 . . . | 72 | 100 | 18.1 | 61.1 | 16.7 | 26.4 | | 1.4 | 5.6 |
| 55 and over . | 94 | 100 | 8.5 | 26.6 | 55.3 | 18.1 | 12.8 | | 5.3 |
| Male | 168 | 100 | 78.2 | 4.8 | 10.1 | 3.2 | 1.6 | .5 | 6.4 |
| 16 - 19 . . . | 82 | 100 | 97.6 | 2.4 | | | | | |
| 20 - 24 . . . | 28 | 100 | 82.1 | 10.7 | | | | | 7.1 |
| 25 - 34 . . . | 29 | 100 | 82.8 | | 3.4 | 3.6 | | | 13.8 |
| 35 - 44 . . . | 11 | 100 | 81.8 | 9.1 | 9.1 | 3.4 | | | |
| 45 - 54 . . . | 13 | 100 | 53.8 | 7.7 | 15.4 | 7.7 | | 7.7 | 23.1 |
| 55 and over . | 25 | 100 | 16.0 | 8.0 | 60.0 | 12.0 | 12.0 | | 12.0 |
| Female | 424 | 100 | 36.3 | 50.7 | 14.6 | 14.9 | 2.8 | .2 | 1.7 |
| 16 - 19 . . . | 90 | 100 | 92.2 | 8.9 | 1.1 | 1.1 | | | 1.8 |
| 20 - 24 . . . | 57 | 100 | 43.9 | 47.4 | 7.0 | 5.3 | 3.5 | | 2.2 |
| 25 - 34 . . . | 90 | 100 | 23.3 | 80.0 | 6.7 | 17.8 | 1.1 | 1.1 | 1.7 |
| 35 - 44 . . . | 59 | 100 | 25.4 | 71.2 | 6.8 | 18.6 | | | |
| 45 - 54 . . . | 59 | 100 | 10.2 | 72.9 | 16.9 | 30.5 | | | 1.7 |
| 55 and over . | 69 | 100 | 5.8 | 33.3 | 53.6 | 20.3 | 13.0 | | 2.9 |

*Percentages add up to more than 100 because a person may have more than one reason.

TABLE C.3.4

EMPLOYMENT STATUS OF PERSONS 16 YEARS OF AGE AND
OLDER BY SEX AND LENGTH OF TIME SINCE DEPARTURE FROM CAMP

| Sex and Length of Time Since Camp Departure | Total | | Employed | Unemployed |
|---|---|---|---|---|
| | N | % | | |
| Total | 1091 | 100 | 87.5 | 12.5 |
| 6 months, less than 7 . . | 17 | 100 | 47.1 | 52.9 |
| 7 months, less than 8 . . | 80 | 100 | 86.3 | 13.8 |
| 8 months, less than 9 . . | 97 | 100 | 85.6 | 14.4 |
| 9 months, less than 10 . . | 151 | 100 | 84.1 | 15.9 |
| 10 months or more . . . . | 746 | 100 | 89.5 | 10.5 |
| Male | 764 | 100 | 89.9 | 10.1 |
| 6 months, less than 7 . . | 12 | 100 | 58.3 | 41.7 |
| 7 months, less than 8 . . | 60 | 100 | 90.0 | 10.0 |
| 8 months, less than 9 . . | 69 | 100 | 85.5 | 14.5 |
| 9 months, less than 10 . . | 104 | 100 | 84.6 | 15.4 |
| 10 months or more . . . . | 519 | 100 | 92.3 | 7.7 |
| Female | 327 | 100 | 82.0 | 18.0 |
| 6 months, less than 7 . . | 5 | 100 | 20.0 | 80.0 |
| 7 months, less than 8 . . | 20 | 100 | 75.0 | 25.0 |
| 8 months, less than 9 . . | 28 | 100 | 85.7 | 14.3 |
| 9 months, less than 10 . . | 47 | 100 | 83.0 | 17.0 |
| 10 months or more . . . . | 227 | 100 | 83.3 | 16.7 |

TABLE C.3.5

EMPLOYMENT STATUS OF PERSONS 16 YEARS AND OLDER BY SEX AND
RELATIONSHIP TO HEADS OF HOUSEHOLD

| Relationship to Household Head | MALE | | | | FEMALE | | | |
|---|---|---|---|---|---|---|---|---|
| | N | % | Employed | Unemployed | N | % | Employed | Unemployed |
| Total . . . . . . | 764 | 100 | 89.9 | 10.1 | 327 | 100 | 82.0 | 18.0 |
| Head . . . . . . | 489 | 100 | 90.6 | 9.4 | 47 | 100 | 91.5 | 8.5 |
| Spouse . . . . . | 5 | 100 | 100.0 | | 131 | 100 | 77.9 | 22.1 |
| Child or spouse . | 107 | 100 | 89.7 | 10.3 | 73 | 100 | 86.3 | 13.7 |
| Grandchild/ nephew/niece . | 9 | 100 | 88.9 | 11.1 | 9 | 100 | 66.7 | 33.3 |
| Parent or spouse. | 10 | 100 | 80.0 | 20.0 | 7 | 100 | 42.9 | 57.1 |
| Other relative. . | 72 | 100 | 83.3 | 16.7 | 59 | 100 | 84.7 | 15.3 |
| Unrelated/no answer . . . . . | 72 | 100 | 93.1 | 6.9 | 1 | 100 | 100.0 | |

## TABLE C.3.6

### EMPLOYMENT STATUS OF PERSONS 16 YEARS AND OLDER BY AGE AND SEX

| Age | MALE | | | | FEMALE | | | |
|---|---|---|---|---|---|---|---|---|
| | N | % | Employed | Unemployed | N | % | Employed | Unemployed |
| Total . . . . . | 764 | 100 | 89.9 | 10.1 | 327 | 100 | 82.0 | 18.0 |
| 16 - 24 . . . . | 234 | 100 | 88.0 | 12.0 | 109 | 100 | 84.4 | 15.6 |
| 25 - 34 . . . . | 270 | 100 | 91.9 | 8.1 | 121 | 100 | 82.6 | 17.4 |
| 35 - 44 . . . . | 152 | 100 | 92.8 | 7.2 | 67 | 100 | 83.6 | 16.4 |
| 45 - 54 . . . . | 78 | 100 | 87.2 | 12.8 | 26 | 100 | 69.2 | 30.8 |
| 55 and over | 30 | 100 | 80.0 | 20.0 | 4 | 100 | 50.0 | 50.0 |

141

TABLE C.3.7

JOB TENURE BY AGE AND SEX

| Age and Sex | Total N | Total % | Less than 1 month | 1 mo. less than 2 | 2 mos. less than 3 | Job Tenure 3 mos. less than 4 | 4 mos. less than 5 | 5 mos. less than 6 | 6 mos. and over | Not Available |
|---|---|---|---|---|---|---|---|---|---|---|
| Total | 955 | 100 | 11.0 | 6.6 | 9.4 | 6.8 | 5.4 | 9.1 | 48.7 | 3.0 |
| 16 – 19 | 106 | 100 | 23.6 | 9.4 | 6.6 | 6.6 | 1.9 | 6.6 | 29.2 | 16.1 |
| 20 – 24 | 192 | 100 | 13.0 | 7.3 | 12.5 | 8.3 | 4.2 | 8.9 | 41.7 | 4.1 |
| 25 – 34 | 348 | 100 | 9.2 | 6.3 | 6.9 | 6.3 | 7.2 | 10.3 | 52.9 | .9 |
| 35 – 44 | 197 | 100 | 6.6 | 5.1 | 9.6 | 6.6 | 3.6 | 9.6 | 58.9 | |
| 45 – 54 | 86 | 100 | 10.5 | 4.7 | 14.0 | 5.8 | 8.1 | 5.8 | 51.2 | |
| 55 and over | 26 | 100 | 3.8 | 11.5 | 15.4 | 7.7 | 11.5 | 11.5 | 38.5 | |
| Male | 687 | 100 | 10.8 | 5.8 | 8.4 | 6.8 | 6.3 | 9.9 | 49.1 | 2.9 |
| 16 – 19 | 69 | 100 | 26.1 | 8.7 | 4.3 | 5.8 | 2.9 | 7.2 | 26.1 | 18.9 |
| 20 – 24 | 137 | 100 | 15.3 | 7.3 | 12.4 | 8.0 | 5.1 | 8.0 | 39.4 | 4.5 |
| 25 – 34 | 248 | 100 | 8.9 | 5.2 | 5.6 | 6.9 | .7 | 12.1 | 53.2 | .4 |
| 35 – 44 | 141 | 100 | 5.0 | 4.3 | 9.2 | 6.4 | 4.3 | 9.9 | 61.0 | |
| 45 – 54 | 68 | 100 | 7.4 | 2.9 | 13.2 | 5.9 | 8.8 | 7.4 | 54.4 | |
| 55 and over | 24 | 100 | 4.2 | 12.5 | 8.3 | 8.3 | 12.5 | 12.5 | 41.7 | |
| Female | 258 | 100 | 11.6 | 8.6 | 11.9 | 6.7 | 3.4 | 7.1 | 47.8 | 2.9 |
| 16 – 19 | 37 | 100 | 18.9 | 10.8 | 10.8 | 8.1 | | 5.4 | 35.1 | 10.9 |
| 20 – 24 | 55 | 100 | 7.3 | 7.3 | 12.7 | 9.1 | 1.8 | 10.9 | 47.3 | 3.6 |
| 25 – 34 | 100 | 100 | 10.0 | 9.0 | 10.0 | 5.0 | 6.0 | 6.0 | 52.0 | 2.0 |
| 35 – 44 | 56 | 100 | 10.7 | 7.1 | 16.7 | 7.1 | 1.8 | | 53.6 | |
| 45 – 54 | 18 | 100 | 22.2 | 11.1 | | 5.6 | 5.6 | 8.9 | 38.9 | |
| 55 and over | 2 | 100 | | | 100.0 | | | | | |

TABLE C.3.8

HOURS WORKED PER WEEK BY AGE AND SEX

| Age and Sex | Total | | Less than 15 | 15-29 | 30-39 | 40 or more |
|---|---|---|---|---|---|---|
| | N | % | | | | |
| Total . . . . . | 955 | 100 | 2.5 | 10.5 | 7.3 | 79.7 |
| 16 – 19 . . . . | 106 | 100 | 10.4 | 32.1 | 7.5 | 50.0 |
| 20 – 24 . . . . | 192 | 100 | 2.6 | 10.9 | 4.2 | 82.3 |
| 25 – 34 . . . . | 348 | 100 | 1.1 | 5.7 | 9.5 | 83.6 |
| 35 – 44 . . . . | 197 | 100 | 1.5 | 8.1 | 7.1 | 83.2 |
| 45 – 54 . . . . | 86 | 100 | 1.2 | 8.1 | 7.0 | 83.7 |
| 55 and over . . | 26 | 100 | | 7.7 | 3.8 | 88.5 |
| Male. . . . . | 687 | 100 | 1.7 | 10.3 | 5.5 | 82.4 |
| 16 – 19 . . . . | 69 | 100 | 8.7 | 37.7 | 2.9 | 50.7 |
| 20 – 24 . . . . | 137 | 100 | 2.2 | 12.4 | 2.2 | 83.2 |
| 25 – 34 . . . . | 248 | 100 | .4 | 5.2 | 7.3 | 87.1 |
| 35 – 44 . . . . | 141 | 100 | .7 | 6.4 | 7.1 | 85.8 |
| 45 – 54 . . . . | 68 | 100 | 1.5 | 5.9 | 5.9 | 86.8 |
| 55 and over . . | 24 | 100 | | 8.3 | 4.2 | 87.5 |
| Female . . . . | 268 | 100 | 4.5 | 10.8 | 11.9 | 72.8 |
| 16 – 19 . . . . | 37 | 100 | 13.5 | 21.6 | 16.2 | 48.6 |
| 20 – 24 . . . . | 55 | 100 | 3.6 | 7.3 | 9.1 | 80.0 |
| 25 – 34 . . . . | 100 | 100 | 3.0 | 7.0 | 15.0 | 75.0 |
| 35 – 44 . . . . | 56 | 100 | 3.6 | 12.5 | 7.1 | 76.8 |
| 45 – 54 . . . . | 18 | 100 | | 16.7 | 11.1 | 72.2 |
| 55 and over . . | 2 | 100 | | | | 100.0 |

TABLE C.3.9

HOURS WORKED PER WEEK BY WEEKLY WAGES AND SALARY INCOME

| Hours per Week | Total | | Weekly Wages and Salary Income | | | | |
|---|---|---|---|---|---|---|---|
| | N | % | Less than $50 | $50 - 99 | $100 - 199 | $200 - more | N/A |
| Total | 955 | 100 | 8.0 | 27.6 | 57.6 | 5.3 | 1.5 |
| Less than 15 . . . . . | 24 | 100 | 100.0 | | | | |
| 15 - 29 . . . . . . | 100 | 100 | 46.0 | 51.0 | 3.0 | | |
| 30 - 39 . . . . . . | 70 | 100 | 1.4 | 55.7 | 40.0 | 2.9 | |
| 40 - more . . . . . | 761 | 100 | .7 | 22.9 | 68.2 | 6.4 | 1.8 |

TABLE C.3.10

DEGREE OF JOB SATISFACTION BY AGE AND SEX

| Age and Sex | Total N | Total % | Very Satisfied | Somewhat Satisfied | Not Satisfied | Not Available |
|---|---|---|---|---|---|---|
| Total . . . . . | 955 | 100 | 44.9 | 41.8 | 11.5 | 1.8 |
| 16 – 19 . . . | 106 | 100 | 42.5 | 39.6 | 17.0 | .9 |
| 20 – 24 . . . | 192 | 100 | 43.2 | 46.9 | 8.3 | 1.6 |
| 25 – 34 . . . | 348 | 100 | 46.3 | 40.2 | 11.8 | 1.7 |
| 35 – 44 . . . | 197 | 100 | 46.2 | 41.1 | 11.2 | 1.5 |
| 45 – 54 . . . | 86 | 100 | 39.5 | 41.9 | 14.0 | 4.7 |
| 55 and over. . | 26 | 100 | 57.7 | 38.5 | 3.8 | |
| Male . . . . . | 687 | 100 | 42.5 | 42.5 | 13.1 | 1.9 |
| 16 – 19 . . . | 69 | 100 | 44.9 | 34.8 | 18.8 | 1.4 |
| 20 – 24 . . . | 137 | 100 | 38.7 | 51.1 | 8.8 | 1.5 |
| 25 – 34 . . . | 248 | 100 | 42.3 | 41.5 | 14.1 | 2.0 |
| 35 – 44 . . . | 141 | 100 | 44.7 | 41.8 | 12.1 | 1.4 |
| 45 – 54 . . . | 68 | 100 | 38.2 | 39.7 | 17.6 | 4.4 |
| 55 and over. . | 24 | 100 | 58.3 | 37.5 | 4.2 | |
| Female . . . . | 268 | 100 | 51.1 | 39.9 | 7.5 | 1.5 |
| 16 – 19 . . . | 37 | 100 | 37.8 | 48.6 | 13.5 | |
| 20 – 24 . . . | 55 | 100 | 54.5 | 36.4 | 7.3 | 1.8 |
| 25 – 34 . . . | 100 | 100 | 56.0 | 37.0 | 6.0 | 1.0 |
| 35 – 44 . . . | 56 | 100 | 50.0 | 39.3 | 8.9 | 1.8 |
| 45 – 54 . . . | 18 | 100 | 44.4 | 50.0 | | 5.6 |
| 55 and over. . | 2 | 100 | 50.0 | 50.0 | | |

145

TABLE C.3.11

REASONS FOR JOB DISSATISFACTION BY SEX AND DEGREE
OF DISSATISFACTION

| Degree of Dissatisfaction | Total N | Total % | Reasons For Job Dissatisfaction* Work Too Demanding | Low Salary | Irregular Schedule | Not in Line With Training | Temporary Job | No Possibility for Advancement | Other |
|---|---|---|---|---|---|---|---|---|---|
| Total | 509 | 100 | 25.7 | 31.4 | 9.4 | 48.5 | 36.1 | 36.9 | 2.9 |
| Somewhat satisfied . . | 399 | 100 | 21.6 | 31.8 | 6.8 | 48.6 | 34.6 | 36.1 | 2.8 |
| Not satisfied . . . | 110 | 100 | 40.9 | 30.0 | 19.1 | 48.2 | 41.8 | 40.0 | 3.6 |
| Male | 382 | 100 | 27.0 | 30.6 | 9.4 | 50.3 | 36.4 | 36.9 | 3.4 |
| Somewhat satisfied . . | 292 | 100 | 23.3 | 30.5 | 6.5 | 50.7 | 35.3 | 37.0 | 3.1 |
| Not satisfied . . . | 90 | 100 | 38.9 | 31.1 | 18.9 | 48.9 | 40.0 | 36.7 | 4.4 |
| Female | 127 | 100 | 22.0 | 33.9 | 9.4 | 43.3 | 35.4 | 37.0 | 1.6 |
| Somewhat satisfied . . | 107 | 100 | 16.8 | 35.5 | 7.5 | 43.0 | 32.7 | 33.6 | 1.9 |
| Not satisfied . . . | 20 | 100 | 50.0 | 25.0 | 20.0 | 45.0 | 50.0 | 55.0 | |

* Percentages add up to more than 100 because a person may have more than one reason.

TABLE C.3.12

EMPLOYMENT STATUS OF HEADS OF HOUSEHOLD
BY VIETNAM OCCUPATION

| Vietnam Occupation | Total | | Employed | Unemployed |
|---|---|---|---|---|
| | N | % | | |
| Total . . . . . . | 536 | 100 | 90.7 | 9.3 |
| White Collar . . . | 359 | 100 | 92.0 | 8.0 |
| Professional . . . | 174 | 100 | 90.8 | 9.2 |
| Managers . . . . . | 95 | 100 | 95.8 | 4.2 |
| Clerical and Sales. | 90 | 100 | 90.0 | 10.0 |
| Blue Collar . . . . | 152 | 100 | 88.8 | 11.2 |
| Craftsman . . . . . | 47 | 100 | 85.1 | 14.9 |
| Operatives and Transport . . . | 15 | 100 | 100.0 | - |
| Laborers . . . . . | 64 | 100 | 92.2 | 7.8 |
| Other Blue Collar . | 26 | 100 | 80.8 | 19.2 |
| Not Ascertained . . | 25 | 100 | 84.0 | 16.0 |

147

TABLE C.3.13

PRESENT OCCUPATION OF HEADS OF HOUSEHOLD BY VIETNAM OCCUPATION

| Vietnam Occupation | Total | | Present Occupation | | | | | | |
| | | | White Collar | | | Blue Collar | | | |
| | N | % | Profes- sional | Mana- gers | Clerical and Sales | Crafts- man | Operatives Transport | Labor- ers | Other Blue Collar |
|---|---|---|---|---|---|---|---|---|---|
| Total . . . . . . | 486 | 100 | 6.2 | 1.4 | 16.5 | 33.1 | 3.9 | 7.2 | 31.7 |
| White Collar . . . | 330 | 100 | 9.1 | 2.1 | 21.8 | 31.8 | 4.5 | 6.7 | 24.0 |
| Professional . . . | 158 | 100 | 14.6 | .6 | 22.8 | 34.8 | 4.4 | 2.5 | 20.3 |
| Managers . . . | 91 | 100 | 3.3 | 4.4 | 17.6 | 25.3 | 7.7 | 12.1 | 29.6 |
| Clerical and Sales . | 81 | 100 | 4.9 | 2.5 | 24.7 | 33.3 | 1.2 | 8.6 | 24.7 |
| Blue Collar . . . | 135 | 100 | | | 6.0 | 39.3 | 3.0 | 9.6 | 42.1 |
| Craftsman . . . . | 40 | 100 | | | 7.5 | 45.0 | 2.5 | 10.0 | 35.0 |
| Operatives and Transport . . . | 15 | 100 | | | | 40.0 | 13.3 | 20.0 | 26.6 |
| Laborers . . . . | 59 | 100 | | | 3.4 | 40.7 | 1.7 | 5.1 | 49.1 |
| Other Blue Collar. | 21 | 100 | | | 4.8 | 23.8 | | 14.3 | 57.1 |
| Not Ascertained . . | 21 | 100 | | | 9.5 | 14.3 | | | 76.2 |

TABLE C.3.14

SATISFACTION OF HEADS OF HOUSEHOLD WITH JOB BY COMPARISON
OF VIETNAM OCCUPATION TO PRESENT OCCUPATION

| Level of Present Employment | Total | | Very Satisfied | Somewhat Satisfied | Not Satisfied | Not Available |
|---|---|---|---|---|---|---|
| | N | % | | | | |
| Total . . . . . . . . | 486 | 100 | 44.2 | 41.8 | 12.3 | 1.6 |
| Presently employed at lower level . . | 329 | 100 | 38.6 | 45.0 | 14.6 | 1.8 |
| Presently employed at comparable level . . . . . . | 77 | 100 | 59.7 | 31.2 | 9.1 | – |
| Presently employed at higher level . . . . | 57 | 100 | 59.6 | 29.8 | 7.0 | 3.5 |

TABLE C.3.15

NUMBER OF JOBS HEADS OF HOUSEHOLD HAVE HELD
BY SEX AND EMPLOYMENT STATUS

| Sex and Employment Status | Total | | Number of Jobs Held | | | | | |
|---|---|---|---|---|---|---|---|---|
| | N | % | None | One | Two | Three | Four | Five |
| Total | 615 | 100 | 11.2 | 58.0 | 18.5 | 8.1 | 1.9 | 1.1 |
| Employed . . . . . | 486 | 100 | – | 63.0 | 22.0 | 9.9 | 2.5 | 1.2 |
| Unemployed . . . . | 50 | 100 | 34.0 | 56.0 | 6.0 | 2.0 | – | 2.0 |
| Not in labor force | 79 | 100 | 65.8 | 27.8 | 5.1 | 1.3 | – | – |
| Male | 545 | 100 | 9.0 | 58.4 | 19.0 | 8.8 | 2.2 | 1.3 |
| Employed . . . . . | 443 | 100 | – | 61.9 | 22.1 | 10.4 | 2.7 | 1.4 |
| Unemployed . . . . | 46 | 100 | 34.8 | 56.5 | 4.3 | 2.2 | – | 2.2 |
| Not in labor force | 56 | 100 | 58.9 | 32.1 | 7.1 | 1.8 | – | – |
| Female | 70 | 100 | 28.2 | 54.9 | 14.1 | 2.8 | – | – |
| Employed . . . . . | 43 | 100 | – | 74.4 | 20.9 | 4.7 | – | – |
| Unemployed . . . . | 4 | 100 | 25.0 | 50.0 | 25.0 | – | – | – |
| Not in labor force | 23 | 100 | 82.6 | 17.4 | – | – | – | – |

150

TABLE C.3.16

CHILDREN ENROLLED IN SCHOOL BY TYPE OF SCHOOL
AND AGE AND SEX

| Age and Sex | Total | | Not Attending School | Day Care or Nursery School | Elementary School | Secondary School | Other |
|---|---|---|---|---|---|---|---|
| | N | % | | | | | |
| Total | 1363 | 100 | 19.4 | 2.2 | 36.2 | 29.9 | 12.2 |
| 3 - 4 . . . . | 174 | 100 | 87.4 | 8.0 | .6 | | 4.0 |
| 5 - 8 . . . . | 349 | 100 | 19.5 | 4.3 | 52.1 | | 24.1 |
| 9 - 12 . . . | 314 | 100 | 1.3 | .3 | 85.4 | 9.9 | 3.2 |
| 13 - 16 . . . | 314 | 100 | 1.3 | | 13.1 | 82.8 | 2.9 |
| 17 - 19 . . . | 212 | 100 | 17.5 | | .9 | 55.2 | 26.4 |
| Male | 706 | 100 | 18.0 | 2.1 | 37.1 | 31.4 | 11.3 |
| 3 - 4 . . . . | 81 | 100 | 90.1 | 7.4 | 1.2 | | 1.2 |
| 5 - 8 . . . . | 180 | 100 | 20.0 | 4.4 | 56.1 | | 19.4 |
| 9 - 12 . . . | 168 | 100 | .6 | .6 | 83.9 | 10.7 | 4.2 |
| 13 - 16 . . . | 163 | 100 | .6 | | 11.0 | 85.9 | 2.5 |
| 17 - 19 . . . | 114 | 100 | 14.0 | | .9 | 56.1 | 28.9 |
| Female | 657 | 100 | 21.0 | 2.3 | 35.3 | 28.3 | 13.1 |
| 3 - 4 . . . . | 93 | 100 | 84.9 | 8.6 | | | 6.5 |
| 5 - 8 . . . . | 169 | 100 | 18.9 | 4.1 | 47.9 | | 29.0 |
| 9 - 12 . . . | 146 | 100 | 2.1 | | 87.0 | 8.9 | 2.1 |
| 13 - 16 . . . | 151 | 100 | 2.0 | | 15.2 | 79.5 | 3.3 |
| 17 - 19 . . . | 98 | 100 | 21.4 | | 1.0 | 54.1 | 23.5 |

151

TABLE C.3.17

ENROLLMENT IN POST SECONDARY EDUCATION BY TYPE OF SCHOOL, AGE, AND SEX

| Age and Sex | Total | | Not Enrolled | College | Type Of School | | | | |
|---|---|---|---|---|---|---|---|---|---|
| | N | % | | | Vocational Tech. Trade | On-The-Job Training | Apprenticeship | Special Program for refugees | Adult Education |
| Total | 1616 | 100 | 62.9 | 8.2 | 5.0 | .3 | 2.4 | 6.6 | 14.5 |
| 17 – 19 . . . . . | 212 | 100 | 73.6 | 12.7 | 3.8 | .5 | .9 | 2.4 | 6.1 |
| 20 – 24 . . . . . | 297 | 100 | 50.2 | 18.9 | 3.7 | .3 | 3.7 | 8.8 | 14.5 |
| 25 – 34 . . . . . | 510 | 100 | 59.4 | 7.5 | 7.3 | .2 | 2.9 | 7.1 | 15.7 |
| 35 – 44 . . . . . | 293 | 100 | 63.5 | 3.4 | 4.1 | .7 | 2.4 | 7.5 | 18.4 |
| 45 and over . . | 304 | 100 | 73.4 | .7 | 4.3 | | 1.0 | 5.9 | 14.8 |
| Male | 902 | 100 | 58.2 | 10.3 | 6.3 | .3 | 3.5 | 6.3 | 15.0 |
| 17 – 19 . . . . . | 114 | 100 | 71.1 | 14.0 | 5.3 | | .9 | 3.5 | 5.3 |
| 20 – 24 . . . . . | 179 | 100 | 46.4 | 20.7 | 3.4 | .6 | 6.1 | 7.3 | 15.6 |
| 25 – 34 . . . . . | 299 | 100 | 56.5 | 10.0 | 8.4 | .3 | 4.0 | 5.4 | 15.4 |
| 35 – 44 . . . . . | 164 | 100 | 61.6 | 4.9 | 5.5 | .6 | 3.7 | 7.9 | 15.9 |
| 45 and over . . | 146 | 100 | 62.3 | 1.4 | 7.5 | | 1.4 | 7.5 | 19.9 |
| Female | 714 | 100 | 68.9 | 5.6 | 3.4 | .3 | .8 | 7.0 | 14.0 |
| 17 – 19 . . . . . | 98 | 100 | 76.5 | 11.2 | 2.0 | | 1.0 | 1.0 | 7.1 |
| 20 – 24 . . . . . | 118 | 100 | 55.9 | 16.1 | 4.2 | 1.0 | | 11.0 | 12.7 |
| 25 – 34 . . . . . | 211 | 100 | 63.5 | 3.8 | 5.7 | | 1.4 | 9.5 | 16.1 |
| 35 – 44 . . . . . | 129 | 100 | 65.9 | 1.6 | 2.3 | .8 | .8 | 7.0 | 21.7 |
| 45 and over . . | 158 | 100 | 83.5 | | 1.3 | | .6 | 4.4 | 10.1 |

TABLE C.3.18

REASONS FOR ATTENDING POST SECONDARY SCHOOLS
BY AGE AND SEX

| Age and Sex | Total | | Reasons for Attending* | | | | |
|---|---|---|---|---|---|---|---|
| | N | % | Improve English Skills | Improve Job Skills | Continue Univ. Education | Other | Not Available |
| Total . . . | 599 | 100 | 56.4 | 22.7 | 19.7 | 1.0 | .2 |
| 17 – 19 . . | 56 | 100 | 33.9 | 21.4 | 44.6 | | |
| 20 – 24 . . | 148 | 100 | 43.9 | 18.2 | 35.8 | 2.0 | |
| 25 – 34 . . | 207 | 100 | 56.0 | 28.0 | 15.0 | 1.0 | |
| 35 – 44 . . | 107 | 100 | 70.1 | 20.6 | 7.5 | .9 | .9 |
| 45 and over . | 81 | 100 | 77.8 | 21.0 | 1.2 | | |
| Male . . . | 377 | 100 | 50.1 | 26.5 | 21.5 | 1.6 | .3 |
| 17 – 19 . . | 33 | 100 | 33.3 | 24.2 | 42.4 | | |
| 20 – 24 . . | 96 | 100 | 39.6 | 21.9 | 35.4 | 3.1 | |
| 25 – 34 . . | 130 | 100 | 47.7 | 30.8 | 20.0 | 1.5 | |
| 35 – 44 . . | 63 | 100 | 60.3 | 27.0 | 9.5 | 1.6 | 1.6 |
| 45 and over . | 55 | 100 | 72.7 | 25.5 | 1.8 | | |
| Female . . . | 222 | 100 | 67.1 | 16.2 | 16.7 | | |
| 17 – 19 . . | 23 | 100 | 34.8 | 17.4 | 47.8 | | |
| 20 – 24 . . | 52 | 100 | 51.9 | 11.5 | 36.5 | | |
| 25 – 34 . . | 77 | 100 | 70.1 | 23.4 | 6.5 | | |
| 35 – 44 . . | 44 | 100 | 84.1 | 11.4 | 4.5 | | |
| 45 and over . | 26 | 100 | 88.5 | 11.5 | | | |

*Percentages add up to more than 100 because a person may have more than one reason.

153

TABLE C.3.19

MONTHLY HOUSEHOLD INCOME FROM ALL SOURCES
BY TIME SINCE DEPARTURE FROM CAMP

| Length of Time Since Camp Departure | Total | | Monthly Household Income (All Sources) | | | | | |
|---|---|---|---|---|---|---|---|---|
| | N | % | Under $200 | $200 to 399 | $400 to 599 | $600 to 799 | $800 and over | N/A |
| Total . . . . . . . | 617 | 100 | 5.3 | 13.1 | 22.2 | 13.9 | 41.2 | 4.2 |
| 6 months, less than 7 | 9 | 100 | 22.2 | 33.3 | - | 11.1 | 22.2 | 11.1 |
| 7 months, less than 8 | 43 | 100 | 2.3 | 18.6 | 27.9 | 9.3 | 34.9 | 7.0 |
| 8 months, less than 9 | 48 | 100 | 10.4 | - | 20.8 | 14.6 | 52.1 | 2.1 |
| 9 months, less than 10 | 87 | 100 | 5.7 | 10.3 | 17.2 | 17.2 | 43.7 | 5.7 |
| 10 months or more . . . | 430 | 100 | 4.7 | 14.2 | 23.3 | 13.7 | 40.5 | 3.7 |

TABLE C.3.20

MONTHLY WAGES AND SALARY INCOME OF HOUSEHOLD
BY TIME SINCE CAMP DEPARTURE

| Time Since Camp Departure | Total | | Monthly Wages and Salary Income | | | | | | |
|---|---|---|---|---|---|---|---|---|---|
| | N | % | Zero Wages | Under $200 | $200 399 | $400 599 | $600 799 | $800 & Over | N/A |
| Total . . . . . . . . | 617 | 100 | 13.9 | 2.6 | 11.2 | 22.5 | 11.8 | 37.0 | 1.0 |
| 6 months, less than 7 | 9 | 100 | 44.4 | 22.2 | | | 11.1 | 22.2 | |
| 7 months, less than 8 | 43 | 100 | 14.0 | 2.3 | 16.3 | 30.2 | 7.0 | 30.2 | |
| 8 months, less than 9 | 48 | 100 | 14.6 | – | 2.1 | 27.1 | 8.3 | 47.9 | |
| 9 months, less than 10 | 87 | 100 | 13.8 | 3.4 | 10.3 | 20.7 | 14.9 | 36.8 | |
| 10 months or more . . | 430 | 100 | 13.3 | 2.3 | 12.1 | 22.1 | 12.1 | 36.7 | 1.4 |

TABLE C.3.21

TYPES OF FEDERAL ASSISTANCE BY TIME
SINCE DEPARTURE FROM CAMP

| Length of Time Since Camp Departure | Total | | Assistance Received* | | | | | |
| --- | --- | --- | --- | --- | --- | --- | --- | --- |
| | N | % | Non Re-ceived | Food Stamps | Medical Aid | Refugee Financial Assistance | SSI |
| Total . . . . . . . | 617 | 100 | 50.1 | 24.7 | 42.8 | 19.8 | 6.3 |
| 6 months, less than 7. | 9 | 100 | 55.6 | 22.2 | 44.4 | 22.2 | – |
| 7 months, less than 8. | 43 | 100 | 55.8 | 18.6 | 32.6 | 14.0 | 11.6 |
| 8 months, less than 9. | 48 | 100 | 22.9 | 35.4 | 56.3 | 33.3 | 14.6 |
| 9 months, less than 10 | 87 | 100 | 42.5 | 27.6 | 52.9 | 19.5 | 4.6 |
| 10 months or more . . . | 430 | 100 | 53.3 | 23.5 | 40.2 | 18.8 | 5.3 |

* Percentages add up to more than 100 because a family may receive more than one type of assistance. Assistance was reported as being received at the time of the interview.

TABLE C.3.22

TYPES OF FEDERAL ASSISTANCE BY VOLAG

| VOLAG | Total | | Assistance Received* | | | | |
|---|---|---|---|---|---|---|---|
| | N | % | Non Re-ceived | Food Stamps | Medical Aid | Refugee Financial Assistance | SSI |
| Total . . . . . . . | 617 | 100 | 50.1 | 24.7 | 42.8 | 19.8 | 6.3 |
| Church World Service | 88 | 100 | 53.4 | 15.9 | 37.5 | 11.4 | 4.5 |
| International Rescue Committee . . | 84 | 100 | 56.0 | 17.9 | 40.5 | 16.7 | 3.6 |
| Lutheran Immigration and Refugee Service | 105 | 100 | 56.2 | 20.0 | 39.0 | 13.3 | 6.7 |
| United HIAS Service | 26 | 100 | 42.3 | 34.6 | 53.8 | 30.8 | - |
| U.S.C.C. . . . . . | 245 | 100 | 44.5 | 32.2 | 46.1 | 26.1 | 7.8 |
| Other . . . . . . | 55 | 100 | 49.1 | 20.0 | 43.6 | 18.2 | 9.1 |
| No VOLAG . . . . . | 14 | 100 | 64.3 | 21.4 | 35.7 | 14.3 | 7.1 |

* Percentages add up to more than 100 because a family may receive more than one type of assistance. Assistance was reported as being received at the time of the interview.

TABLE C.3.23

RESIDENCE ARRANGEMENTS BY ANNUAL HOUSEHOLD INCOME

| Household Income | Total N | Total % | Purchase Resi- dence | Rent Resi- dence | Resi- dence Lent by Friend | Spon- sor's Resi- dence | Resi- dence of Friend | Rela- tive's Resi- dence | Other |
|---|---|---|---|---|---|---|---|---|---|
| Total . . . . . . | 617 | 100 | 7.5 | 80.7 | 1.6 | 5.2 | 1.3 | 1.3 | 2.4 |
| Under $2,500 (under 200)* . | 33 | 100 | 6.1 | 57.6 | 3.0 | 21.2 | - | 3.0 | 9.1 |
| $2,500 to 4,999 (200-399)* . . | 81 | 100 | 2.5 | 79.0 | 4.9 | 4.9 | 2.5 | - | 6.2 |
| $5,000 to 7,499 (400-599)* . . | 137 | 100 | 5.8 | 82.5 | 2.2 | 4.4 | 2.9 | 1.5 | .7 |
| $7,500 to 9,999 (600-799)* . . | 86 | 100 | 7.0 | 84.9 | - | 3.5 | 2.3 | 2.3 | - |
| $10,000 and over (800 +)* . . . | 254 | 100 | 10.6 | 84.6 | .8 | 2.4 | - | .8 | .8 |

*Equivalent monthly income.

158

TABLE C.3.24

MONTHLY HOUSING COSTS BY RESIDENCE ARRANGEMENT

| Residence Arrangement | Total N | Total % | No Payment | Less than $100 | 101 to 150 | 151 to 200 | 201 to 250 | 251 to 300 | 301 to 350 | 351 or more | No Answer |
|---|---|---|---|---|---|---|---|---|---|---|---|
| Total . . . . . . | 617 | 100 | 9.4 | 19.8 | 24.0 | 24.1 | 13.3 | 5.0 | 2.4 | 1.8 | .2 |
| Separate residence . | 554 | 100 | 3.2 | 19.0 | 26.0 | 26.9 | 14.4 | 5.6 | 2.7 | 2.0 | .2 |
| Own. . . . . . . | 46 | 100 | - | 17.4 | 21.7 | 15.2 | 19.6 | 13.0 | 4.3 | 8.7 | - |
| Rent. . . . . . | 498 | 100 | 1.8 | 19.5 | 26.9 | 28.5 | 14.3 | 4.8 | 2.6 | 1.4 | .2 |
| Lent by friend . . | 10 | 100 | 90.0 | - | - | - | - | 10.0 | - | - | - |
| Sponsor's house . . | 32 | 100 | 71.9 | 15.6 | 6.3 | - | 6.3 | - | - | - | - |
| Friend's house . . | 8 | 100 | 37.5 | 62.5 | - | - | - | - | - | - | - |
| Relative's house . . | 8 | 100 | 62.5 | 12.5 | 25.0 | - | - | - | - | - | - |
| Other . . . . . . | 15 | 100 | 60.0 | 40.0 | - | - | - | - | - | - | - |

TABLE C.3.25

TYPE OF HOUSING BY MONTHLY HOUSING COSTS

| Type of Housing | Total | | No Payment | $100 or less | $101 to 150 | $151 to 200 | $201 to 250 | $251 to 300 | $301 to 350 | $351 or more | No Answer |
| --- | --- | --- | --- | --- | --- | --- | --- | --- | --- | --- | --- |
| | N | % | | | | | | | | | |
| Total . . . . . | 617 | 100 | 9.4 | 19.8 | 24.0 | 24.1 | 13.3 | 5.0 | 2.4 | 1.8 | .2 |
| Detached Home. . | 275 | 100 | 14.9 | 20.0 | 20.0 | 15.3 | 13.8 | 8.7 | 4.0 | 3.3 | — |
| Semi detached. . | 25 | 100 | — | 20.0 | 24.0 | 40.0 | 12.0 | 4.0 | — | — | — |
| Row/town house . | 30 | 100 | 3.3 | 20.0 | 33.3 | 20.0 | 20.0 | — | 3.3 | — | — |
| Apartment . . . | 262 | 100 | 4.6 | 17.9 | 26.7 | 32.8 | 13.4 | 2.3 | 1.1 | .8 | .4 |
| Mobile home. . . | 16 | 100 | — | 31.3 | 43.8 | 25.0 | — | — | — | — | — |
| Other. . . . . . | 9 | 100 | 44.4 | 44.4 | — | 11.1 | — | — | — | — | — |

TABLE C.3.26

EMPLOYMENT STATUS OF PERSONS 16 YEARS AND OLDER
BETWEEN SURVEY I, SURVEY II AND SURVEY III
(Longitudinal)

| Employment Status | Survey I | Survey II | Survey III |
|---|---|---|---|
| Total Households | | | |
| Total Persons | 446 / 738 | 446 / 774 | 398 / 697 |
| Employed . . . . . . | 60.8% | 79.3% | 83.6% |
| Unemployed . . . . . | 39.2 | 20.7 | 16.4 |
| Male | 477 | 489 | 432 |
| Employed . . . . . . | 66.9 | 82.8 | 86.1 |
| Unemployed . . . . . | 33.1 | 17.2 | 13.2 |
| Female | 261 | 285 | 265 |
| Employed . . . . . . | 49.4 | 73.3 | 79.6 |
| Unemployed . . . . . | 50.6 | 26.7 | 20.4 |

TABLE C.3.27

OCCUPATIONAL LEVEL OF EMPLOYED HEADS
BETWEEN SURVEY I, SURVEY II AND SURVEY III
(Longitudinal)

| Type of Occupation | Survey I | | Survey II | | Survey III | |
|---|---|---|---|---|---|---|
| | N | % | N | % | N | % |
| Total | 234 | 100.0 | 301 | 100.0 | 298 | 100.0 |
| White Collar . . . . . . | | | | | | |
| Professional . . . . . | 11 | 4.7 | 33 | 11.0 | 24 | 8.1 |
| Managerial . . . . . | 3 | 1.3 | 6 | 2.0 | 3 | 1.0 |
| Clerical and Sales . . | 43 | 18.4 | 54 | 17.9 | 86 | 28.9 |
| Blue Collar . . . . . . | | | | | | |
| Craftsman . . . . . | 48 | 20.5 | 49 | 16.3 | 99 | 33.2 |
| Operatives and Transport . . . . . | 5 | 2.1 | 19 | 6.3 | 10 | 3.4 |
| Laborers . . . . . | 31 | 13.2 | 43 | 14.3 | 16 | 5.4 |
| Other . . . . . . . | 87 | 37.2 | 97 | 32.2 | 60 | 20.1 |
| Not Ascertained. . . . | 6 | 2.6 | - | - | - | - |

162

TABLE C.3.28

MONTHLY WAGES AND SALARY INCOME OF EMPLOYED PERSONS 16 YEARS
AND OLDER BETWEEN SURVEY I, SURVEY II AND SURVEY III
(Longitudinal)

| Wages and Salary Income | Survey I | Survey II | Survey III |
|---|---|---|---|
| Total | 454 | 618 | 583 |
| Head | 234 | 301 | 298 |
| Zero income . . . . | - | 1.0 | - |
| Less than $200 . . . | 2.6 | 6.3 | 4.7 |
| $200 – $399 . . . | 35.0 | 29.5 | 17.8 |
| $400 – $599 . . . | 40.2 | 37.2 | 35.9 |
| $600 – $799 . . . | 13.7 | 16.0 | 26.2 |
| $800 – over . . . . | 5.1 | 10.0 | 14.8 |
| Not ascertained . . . | 3.4 | - | .6 |
| Other | 220 | 317 | 285 |
| Zero income . . . . | 11.4 | 2.5 | - |
| Less than $200 . . . | - | 14.2 | 10.5 |
| $200 – $399 . . . | 59.5 | 43.5 | 32.3 |
| $400 – $599 . . . | 24.1 | 31.2 | 39.6 |
| $600 – $799 . . . | 2.3 | 6.6 | 11.2 |
| $800 – over . . . . | .9 | 1.9 | 4.2 |
| Not ascertained . . . | 1.8 | - | 2.1 |

163

TABLE C.3.29

FEDERAL ASSISTANCE RECEIVED BY REFUGEE HOUSEHOLDS
BETWEEN SURVEY I, SURVEY II AND SURVEY III
(Longitudinal)

| Type of Federal Assistance * | Survey I | Survey II | Survey III |
|---|---|---|---|
| Total | <u>446</u> | <u>446</u> | <u>398</u> |
| <u>Percentages Receiving</u> | | | |
| Food Stamps . . . . . . . . . . . | 26.0 | 27.6 | 25.3 |
| Medical Aid . . . . . . . . . . | 19.7 | 30.5 | 40.4 |
| Refugee Financial Assistance. . . | 19.1 | 17.3 | 23.6 |
| SSI . . . . . . . . . . . | .4 | 3.1 | 9.7 |

*Assistance was reported as being received at the time of the interview.

164

TABLE C.3.30

LABOR FORCE PARTICIPATION OF VIETNAM REFUGEES
IN SURVEY I, SURVEY II AND SURVEY III BY PROFICIENCY IN ENGLISH
(Cross-Sectional)

| Proficiency In English | Survey I | | | | Survey II | | | | Survey III | | | |
|---|---|---|---|---|---|---|---|---|---|---|---|---|
| | Persons 16 yrs. and older | | In Labor Force | Not In Labor Force | Persons 16 yrs. and older | | In Labor Force | Not In Labor Force | Persons 16 yrs. and older | | In Labor Force | Not In Labor Force |
| | N | % | | | N | % | | | N | % | | |
| Total | 5324 | 100 | 56.1 | 43.9 | 3128 | 100 | 64.0 | 36.0 | 1714 | 100 | 64.1 | 35.9 |
| Understand English | | | | | | | | | | | | |
| Not at all . . . . . . | 549 | 100 | 23.1 | 76.9 | 441 | 100 | 35.1 | 64.9 | 179 | 100 | 26.3 | 73.7 |
| Some . . . . . . | 3340 | 100 | 55.6 | 44.0 | 2192 | 100 | 67.6 | 32.4 | 1201 | 100 | 66.4 | 33.6 |
| Well . . . . . . | 1280 | 100 | 76.2 | 23.8 | 446 | 100 | 81.4 | 18.6 | 334 | 100 | 76.2 | 23.8 |
| Speak English . . . . | | | | | | | | | | | | |
| Not at all . . . . . . | 578 | 100 | 24.4 | 75.6 | 453 | 100 | 35.5 | 64.5 | 181 | 100 | 27.6 | 72.4 |
| Some . . . . . . | 3344 | 100 | 56.0 | 44.4 | 2191 | 100 | 67.7 | 32.3 | 1199 | 100 | 66.2 | 33.8 |
| Well . . . . . . | 1250 | 100 | 75.7 | 24.3 | 437 | 100 | 81.2 | 18.8 | 334 | 100 | 76.5 | 23.5 |
| Read English . . . . | | | | | | | | | | | | |
| Not at all . . . . . . | 589 | 100 | 24.1 | 75.9 | 469 | 100 | 36.9 | 63.1 | 199 | 100 | 29.6 | 70.4 |
| Some . . . . . . | 3235 | 100 | 55.4 | 44.6 | 2131 | 100 | 67.2 | 32.8 | 1167 | 100 | 66.1 | 33.9 |
| Well . . . . . . | 1342 | 100 | 76.3 | 23.7 | 478 | 100 | 82.2 | 17.8 | 348 | 100 | 77.2 | 22.8 |
| Write English . . . . | | | | | | | | | | | | |
| Not at all . . . . . . | 613 | 100 | 25.3 | 74.7 | 477 | 100 | 37.5 | 62.5 | 200 | 100 | 29.5 | 70.5 |
| Some . . . . . . | 3252 | 100 | 55.7 | 44.3 | 2142 | 100 | 67.4 | 32.6 | 1169 | 100 | 66.1 | 33.9 |
| Well . . . . . . | 1304 | 100 | 76.1 | 24.0 | 460 | 100 | 81.7 | 18.3 | 345 | 100 | 77.6 | 22.4 |

TABLE C.3.31

COMPARISON OF DEGREE OF EDUCATIONAL ATTAINMENT FOR LABOR FORCE
PARTICIPANTS IN SURVEY I, SURVEY II AND SURVEY III BY SEX

(Cross-Sectional)

| Educational Attainment | Male | | | | | | Female | | | | | |
|---|---|---|---|---|---|---|---|---|---|---|---|---|
| | Survey I | | Survey II | | Survey III | | Survey I | | Survey II | | Survey III | |
| | N | % | N | % | N | % | N | % | N | % | N | % |
| Total | 1869 | 100.0 | 1499 | 100.0 | 764 | 100.0 | 1113 | 100.0 | 504 | 100.0 | 327 | 100.0 |
| None . . . . . . | 96 | 5.1 | 201 | 13.4 | 221 | 28.9 | 110 | 9.9 | 142 | 28.2 | 140 | 42.8 |
| Primary Diploma . | 71 | 3.8 | 149 | 10.0 | 38 | 4.9 | 90 | 8.1 | 46 | 9.1 | 15 | 4.6 |
| BEPSI/DEPSI/BE . . | 277 | 14.8 | 260 | 17.3 | 93 | 12.2 | 268 | 24.1 | 72 | 14.3 | 34 | 10.4 |
| BACC I . . . . | 178 | 9.5 | 159 | 10.6 | 41 | 5.4 | 131 | 11.8 | 57 | 11.3 | 24 | 7.3 |
| BACC II . . . . | 682 | 36.5 | 554 | 37.0 | 272 | 35.6 | 326 | 29.3 | 148 | 29.4 | 92 | 28.1 |
| University . . . | 480 | 25.7 | 144 | 9.6 | 93 | 12.2 | 148 | 13.3 | 34 | 6.7 | 21 | 6.4 |
| Other . . . . . | 49 | 2.6 | 32 | 2.1 | 6 | .8 | 10 | .9 | 5 | 1.0 | 1 | .3 |
| Not ascertained . | 36 | 1.9 | — | — | — | — | 30 | 2.7 | — | — | — | — |

TABLE C.3.32

EMPLOYMENT OF HOUSEHOLD HEADS AT TIME OF SURVEY I,
SURVEY II AND SURVEY III BY TYPE OF OCCUPATION
(Cross- Sectional)

| Occupation | Survey I | | Survey II | | Survey III | |
|---|---|---|---|---|---|---|
| | N | % | N | % | N | % |
| Total | 897 | 100.0 | 725 | 100.0 | 486 | 100.0 |
| White Collar | | | | | | |
| Professional . . . . | 64 | 7.1 | 35 | 4.8 | 158 | 32.5 |
| Managerial . . . . . | 13 | 1.4 | 4 | .6 | 91 | 18.7 |
| Clerical and Sales . | 175 | 19.5 | 81 | 11.2 | 81 | 16.7 |
| Blue Collar | | | | | | |
| Craftsman . . . . | 146 | 16.3 | 176 | 24.3 | 40 | 8.2 |
| Operatives and | | | | | | |
| Transport. . . . . | 24 | 2.7 | 45 | 6.2 | 15 | 3.1 |
| Laborers . . . . . | 108 | 12.1 | 128 | 17.6 | 59 | 12.1 |
| Other . . . . . . | 307 | 34.2 | 256 | 35.3 | 21 | 4.3 |
| Not Ascertained | 60 | 6.7 | - | - | 21 | 4.3 |

167

TABLE C.3.33

## DISTRIBUTION OF REFUGEE HOUSEHOLDS
## BY REGION
(Cross-Sectional)

| Region | N | % |
|--------|-----|-------|
| Total | 617 | 100.0 |
| North-eastern Region . . . . . | 89 | 14.4 |
| Western Region . . . . . . | 184 | 29.8 |
| North-central Region . . . . . | 165 | 26.7 |
| Southern Region . . . . . . | 179 | 29.0 |

168

TABLE C.3.34

DISTRIBUTION OF REFUGES BY AGE AND SEX

(Cross-Sectional)

| Age and Sex | N | % |
|---|---|---|
| Total | 2932 | 100.0 |
| Male | 1580 | 53.8 |
| 0 – 4 . . . . . . | 167 | 5.7 |
| 5 – 14 . . . . . . | 420 | 14.3 |
| 15 – 24 . . . . . . | 384 | 13.1 |
| 25 – 34 . . . . . . | 299 | 10.2 |
| 35 – 44 . . . . . . | 164 | 5.6 |
| 45 – 54 . . . . . . | 91 | 3.1 |
| 55 – 64 . . . . . . | 40 | 1.4 |
| 65 and over . . . | 15 | .5 |
| Female | 1352 | 46.1 |
| 0 – 4 . . . . . . | 172 | 5.9 |
| 5 – 14 . . . . . . | 380 | 12.9 |
| 15 – 24 . . . . . . | 302 | 10.3 |
| 25 – 34 . . . . . . | 211 | 7.2 |
| 35 – 44 . . . . . . | 129 | 4.4 |
| 45 – 54 . . . . . . | 85 | 2.9 |
| 55 – 64 . . . . . . | 37 | 1.3 |
| 65 and over . . . | 36 | 1.2 |

TABLE C.4.1

LABOR FORCE PARTICIPATION OF PERSONS 16 YEARS AND
OLDER BY SEX
(Cross-sectional)
(Weighted Percentages)

| Sex | Unweighted N | In Labor Force | | Not in Labor Force |
|---|---|---|---|---|
| | | Employed | Not Employed | |
| Total . . . . . . | 1686 | 57.6 | 4.9 | 37.5 |
| Males . . . . . | 932 | 72.4 | 4.1 | 23.6 |
| Females . . . . | 754 | 38.5 | 6.0 | 55.5 |

## TABLE C.4.2

### LABOR FORCE PARTICIPATION OF PERSONS 16 YEARS AND OLDER BY SEX AND RELATIONSHIP TO HEAD OF HOUSEHOLD
#### (Cross-sectional)
#### (Weighted Percentages)

| Relationship to Household Head | Males | | | | Females | | | |
|---|---|---|---|---|---|---|---|---|
| | Unweighted N | In Labor Force | | Not in Labor Force | Unweighted N | In Labor Force | | Not in Labor Force |
| | | Employed | Not Employed | | | Employed | Not Employed | |
| Total . . . . . . . . | 932 | 72.4 | 4.1 | 23.6 | 754 | 38.5 | 6.0 | 55.5 |
| Head . . . . . . . . | 570 | 81.3 | 5.4 | 13.3 | 75 | 58.4 | 10.0 | 31.5 |
| Spouse . . . . . . . | 9 | 90.6 | - | 9.4 | 361 | 39.0 | 7.0 | 54.1 |
| Child or spouse. . . | 175 | 40.8 | 2.0 | 57.3 | 157 | 31.4 | 2.7 | 65.9 |
| Grandchild nephew/niece . . | 16 | 73.9 | - | 26.1 | 11 | 46.8 | - | 53.2 |
| Parent or spouse . . | 22 | 39.6 | - | 60.4 | 65 | 6.4 | 3.0 | 90.6 |
| Other relative . . | 89 | 58.7 | 1.9 | 39.4 | 82 | 52.7 | 6.0 | 41.3 |
| Unrelated/no answer . . . . . | 51 | 93.9 | 3.0 | 3.1 | 3 | 19.9 | 19.9 | 60.2 |

171

## TABLE C.4.3

### REASONS FOR NOT SEEKING EMPLOYMENT BY AGE AND SEX
(Cross-sectional)
(Weighted Percentages)

| Age and Sex | Unweighted N | Reasons Given | | | | | | |
|---|---|---|---|---|---|---|---|---|
| | | Attending School | Keeping House | Poor Health | Can Not Speak English | Other Means of Support | Dis-couraged | Other |
| Total . . . . . . | 663 | 56.0 | 28.2 | 17.7 | 14.9 | 1.6 | .1 | 2.1 |
| 16-24. . . . . | 302 | 86.2 | 10.8 | 2.0 | 3.0 | 1.6 | - | 1.6 |
| 25-34. . . . . | 121 | 45.2 | 60.2 | 6.9 | 10.0 | .7 | .7 | 2.2 |
| 35-44. . . . . | 69 | 44.7 | 50.4 | 6.4 | 22.3 | 1.2 | - | 4.0 |
| 45 and over. . | 171 | 13.8 | 26.8 | 59.1 | 37.0 | 2.4 | - | 2.4 |
| Males. . . . . | 227 | 83.7 | - | 12.2 | 3.1 | 2.1 | - | 5.0 |
| 16-24. . . . . | 138 | 96.6 | - | .6 | - | 2.3 | - | 2.2 |
| 25-34. . . . . | 33 | 92.2 | - | 7.7 | - | - | - | 5.1 |
| 35-44. . . . . | 13 | 94.1 | - | 5.9 | - | - | - | 18.9 |
| 45 and over. . | 43 | 34.6 | - | 53.0 | 16.1 | 3.5 | - | 8.8 |
| Females. . . . . | 436 | 40.9 | 43.6 | 20.7 | 21.2 | 1.3 | .2 | .6 |
| 16-24. . . . . | 164 | 77.3 | 20.1 | 3.2 | 5.5 | 1.0 | - | 1.0 |
| 25-34. . . . . | 88 | 27.5 | 82.9 | 6.6 | 13.8 | .9 | 1.0 | 1.0 |
| 35-44. . . . . | 56 | 31.3 | 64.1 | 6.5 | 28.3 | 1.5 | - | - |
| 45 and over. . | 128 | 6.0 | 36.9 | 61.4 | 44.9 | 2.0 | - | - |

**TABLE C.4.4**

EMPLOYMENT STATUS OF PERSONS 16 YEARS AND OLDER BY SEX AND
RELATIONSHIP TO HEAD OF HOUSEHOLD
(Cross-sectional)
(Weighted Percentages)

| Relationship to Household Head | Males | | | Females | | |
|---|---|---|---|---|---|---|
| | Unweighted N | Employed | Not Employed | Unweighted N | Employed | Not Employed |
| Total. . . . . . . | 704 | 94.6 | 5.3 | 318 | 86.4 | 13.6 |
| Head . . . . . . . | 497 | 93.8 | 6.2 | 50 | 85.4 | 14.6 |
| Spouse . . . . . . | 8 | 100.0 | - | 160 | 84.8 | 15.2 |
| Child or spouse. . | 76 | 95.4 | 4.6 | 52 | 92.0 | 8.0 |
| Grandchild/ nephew/niece . . | 10 | 100.0 | - | 4 | 100.0 | - |
| Parent or spouse . | 8 | 100.0 | - | 5 | 68.0 | 32.0 |
| Other relative . . | 56 | 96.9 | 3.1 | 45 | 89.8 | 10.2 |
| Unrelated/no answer . . . . | 49 | 96.9 | 3.1 | 2 | 50.0 | 50.0 |

173

TABLE C.4.5

EMPLOYMENT STATUS OF PERSONS 16 YEARS
AND OLDER BY AGE AND SEX
(Cross-sectional)
(Weighted Percentages)

| Age and Sex | Unweighted N | Employed | Not Employed |
|---|---|---|---|
| Total. . . . . . | 1022 | 92.1 | 7.9 |
| 16-24. . . . : | 283 | 94.4 | 5.6 |
| 25-34. . . . : | 372 | 92.8 | 7.2 |
| 35-44. . . . : | 219 | 90.4 | 9.6 |
| 45-over. . . : | 148 | 87.9 | 12.1 |
| Males. . . . . | 704 | 94.6 | 5.4 |
| 16-24. . . . : | 197 | 97.1 | 2.9 |
| 25-34. . . . : | 246 | 95.3 | 4.7 |
| 35-44. . . . : | 146 | 93.5 | 6.5 |
| 45-over. . . : | 115 | 90.1 | 9.9 |
| Females. . . . | 318 | 86.4 | 13.6 |
| 16-24. . . . : | 86 | 88.2 | 11.8 |
| 25-34. . . . : | 126 | 87.9 | 12.1 |
| 35-44. . . . : | 73 | 84.0 | 16.0 |
| 45-over. . . : | 33 | 80.3 | 19.7 |

TABLE C.4.6

JOB-HUNTING METHODS OF UNEMPLOYED REFUGEES BY SEX
(Cross-sectional)
(Weighted Percentages)

| Sex | Unweighted N | % | Job-Hunting Methods* | | | | | | |
| | | | Contact Employ- er | Contact Employ- ment Agencies | Through Friend/ Rela- tive | Through Sponsor | Answer Ads | Place Ads | Other |
|---|---|---|---|---|---|---|---|---|---|
| Total. . . | 82 | 100.0 | 58.1 | 60.3 | 37.2 | 23.7 | 27.1 | 5.2 | 1.8 |
| Males. . | 40 | 100.0 | 58.2 | 67.4 | 40.8 | 41.4 | 38.2 | 4.4 | 2.0 |
| Females. | 42 | 100.0 | 58.1 | 54.0 | 34.2 | 8.2 | 17.3 | 6.0 | 1.8 |

*Each person may use more than one of these methods in job-hunting.

175

## TABLE C.4.7

### JOB-HUNTING METHODS OF UNEMPLOYED REFUGEES BY AGE
#### (Cross-sectional)
#### (Weighted Percentages)

| Age | Unweighted N | % | Job-Hunting Methods* | | | | | | |
|---|---|---|---|---|---|---|---|---|---|
| | | | Contact Employer | Contact Employment Agencies | Through Friend/Relative | Through Sponsor | Answer Ads | Place Ads | Other |
| Total. . . | 82 | 100.0 | 58.1 | 60.3 | 37.2 | 23.7 | 27.1 | 5.2 | 1.8 |
| 16-24. . . | 16 | 100.0 | 52.4 | 41.7 | 52.8 | 12.9 | 9.9 | – | – |
| 25-34. . . | 22 | 100.0 | 70.8 | 77.2 | 29.3 | 29.9 | 35.2 | 12.2 | – |
| 35-44. . . | 24 | 100.0 | 58.4 | 54.6 | 41.2 | 8.3 | 37.8 | 4.2 | 3.9 |
| 45-over. . | 20 | 100.0 | 42.2 | 56.4 | 31.3 | 41.4 | 18.0 | – | 4.4 |

*Each person may use more than one of these methods in job-hunting.

TABLE C.4.8

HOURS WORKED PER WEEK BY AGE AND SEX
(Cross-sectional)
(Weighted Percentages)

| Age and Sex | Unweighted N | Hours Worked Per Week | | | | |
|---|---|---|---|---|---|---|
| | | Less than 15 | 15-29 | 30-39 | 40 or more | N/A |
| Total. . . . . | 940 | 1.9 | 10.1 | 7.7 | 80.0 | .2 |
| 16-24. . . . | 267 | 4.9 | 20.7 | 6.2 | 67.6 | .7 |
| 25-34. . . . | 350 | 1.2 | 5.4 | 8.7 | 84.7 | - |
| 35-44. . . . | 195 | .4 | 6.1 | 8.4 | 85.1 | - |
| 45-over. . . | 128 | - | 6.7 | 7.2 | 86.0 | - |
| Males. . . . | 664 | 1.9 | 9.5 | 7.9 | 80.5 | .3 |
| 16-24. . . . | 191 | 4.4 | 23.6 | 5.9 | 65.1 | 1.0 |
| 25-34. . . . | 235 | 1.4 | 4.5 | 8.6 | 85.5 | - |
| 35-44. . . . | 135 | .6 | 3.3 | 9.0 | 87.1 | - |
| 45-over. . . | 103 | - | 2.3 | 8.3 | 89.4 | - |
| Females. . . | 276 | 2.0 | 11.7 | 7.4 | 78.9 | - |
| 16-24. . . . | 76 | 6.0 | 13.6 | 6.8 | 73.6 | - |
| 25-34. . . . | 115 | .7 | 7.3 | 8.8 | 83.1 | - |
| 35-44. . . . | 60 | - | 12.4 | 7.1 | 80.4 | - |
| 45-over. . . | 25 | - | 24.1 | 3.0 | 72.9 | - |

177

TABLE C.4.9

HOURS WORKED PER WEEK BY WEEKLY WAGES AND
SALARY INCOME
(Cross-sectional)
(Weighted Percentages)

| Hours per Week | Unweighted N | Weekly Wages and Salary Income | | | | | |
| | | Less than $50 | $50-99 | $100-199 | $200-more | N/A |
|---|---|---|---|---|---|---|
| Total. . . . . . | 940 | 6.4 | 16.9 | 65.2 | 9.9 | 1.6 |
| Less than 15 . . | 20 | 100.0 | — | — | — | — |
| 15-29. . . . . | 106 | 40.4 | 57.0 | 2.6 | — | — |
| 30-39. . . . | 81 | 1.1 | 39.3 | 53.0 | 6.6 | — |
| 40 or more . . | 732 | .3 | 10.1 | 76.1 | 11.8 | 1.7 |

## TABLE C.4.10

### MONTHLY HOUSEHOLD INCOME FROM ALL SOURCES
(Cross-sectional)
(Weighted Percentages)

| Income Level | Households with Income | |
|---|---|---|
| | Unweighted N | % |
| Total . . . . . . . . . . | 645 | 100.0 |
| Under $200 . . . . . . . | 23 | 3.6 |
| 200 - 399 . . . . . . . | 62 | 9.6 |
| 400 - 599 . . . . . . . | 131 | 20.3 |
| 600 - 799 . . . . . . . | 107 | 16.6 |
| 800 - over. . . . . . . | 305 | 47.3 |
| Not Ascertained . . . . | 17 | 2.6 |

TABLE C.4.11

MONTHLY HOUSEHOLD INCOME FROM ALL SOURCES
BY COMPONENTS OF INCOME
(Cross-sectional)
(Weighted Percentages)

| Household Income (All Sources) | Percent of Households Deriving Income From Each Source | | | | |
|---|---|---|---|---|---|
| | Unweighted N | Wages and Salary Income | Refugee Financial Assistance* | SSI* | Other Financial Contributions* |
| Total . . . . . . . | 645 | 86.4 | 23.4 | 6.5 | 9.3 |
| Under $200 . . . . | 23 | 25.5 | 55.0 | – | 33.2 |
| 200 – 399 . . . . | 62 | 58.5 | 35.7 | 6.9 | 19.3 |
| 400 – 599 . . . . | 131 | 84.7 | 23.0 | 3.6 | 9.1 |
| 600 – 799 . . . . | 107 | 93.5 | 22.7 | 6.0 | 6.9 |
| 800 – over . . . . | 305 | 99.7 | 19.4 | 9.1 | 6.2 |
| Not ascertained. . | 17 | 47.6 | – | – | – |

*Assistance was reported as being received at the time of the interview.

180

## TABLE C.4.12

### MONTHLY HOUSEHOLD INCOME FROM ALL SOURCES
### BY COMPONENTS OF INCOME
(Cross-sectional)
(Weighted Percentages)

| Income Level | Unweighted N | Total Income | Percent of Dollar Contributions From Each Source | | | | |
| --- | --- | --- | --- | --- | --- | --- | --- |
| | | | Contributions by Wages and Salary | Contributions by RFA* | Contributions by SSI* | Contributions by Other* |
| Total. . . . . . . | 645 | $543,871 | 87.9 | 8.2 | 1.4 | 2.5 |
| Under $200 . . . . | 23 | 3,345 | 22.1 | 55.1 | - | 22.8 |
| 200 - 399. . . . . | 62 | 19,227 | 53.9 | 27.2 | 4.5 | 14.3 |
| 400 - 599. . . . . | 131 | 64,566 | 81.6 | 13.3 | 1.3 | 3.8 |
| 600 - 799. . . . . | 107 | 72,293 | 85.0 | 11.5 | 1.1 | 2.3 |
| 800 - over . . . . | 305 | 384,440 | 92.4 | 4.9 | 1.3 | 1.4 |
| Not ascertained. . | 17 | - | - | - | - | - |

*Assistance was reported as being received at the time of the interview.

TABLE C.4.13

TYPES OF FEDERAL ASSISTANCE RECEIVED BY
REFUGEE HOUSEHOLDS

(Comparison Among Surveys I, II, III, and IV)
(Weighted Percentages)

| Type of Assistance | Survey I | Survey II | Survey III | Survey IV |
|---|---|---|---|---|
| Total . . . . . . . . . | 1568 | 1424 | 617 | 645 |
| % Receiving Assistance | 39.6 | 42.0 | 49.9 | 33.4* |
| Food Stamps . . . . . | 21.4 | 25.6 | 24.7 | 24.7 |
| Medical Assistance. . | 17.9 | 23.7 | 42.8 | N/A |
| Refugee Financial Assistance. . . . . | 18.2 | 13.4 | 19.8 | 23.4 |
| SSI . . . . . . . | .5 | 2.8 | 6.3 | 6.5 |
| Other . . . . . . | 1.6 | – | – | – |

*Does not include medical assistance. Information from States
indicates 47.6% of refugees were eligible for medical assistance
as of March 1, 1977; household data are not available.

## TABLE C.4.14

### DISTRIBUTION OF HOUSEHOLDS BY REGION
(Cross-sectional)
(Unweighted Data)

| Region | N | % |
|---|---|---|
| Total. . . . . . . . . . | 645 | 100.0 |
| North-eastern Region . . . | 94 | 14.6 |
| Western Region . . . . | 210 | 32.6 |
| North-central Region . . . | 150 | 23.2 |
| Southern Region. . . . | 191 | 29.6 |

183

TABLE C.4.15

DISTRIBUTION OF REFUGEES BY AGE
(Cross-sectional)
(Unweighted Data)

| Age | N | % |
|---|---|---|
| Total. . . . . . . . . . . . | 2949 | 100.0 |
| 0 - 4. . . . . . | 381 | 12.9 |
| 5 - 14. . . . . . | 804 | 27.3 |
| 15 - 24. . . . . . | 663 | 22.5 |
| 25 - 34. . . . . . | 493 | 16.7 |
| 35 - 44. . . . . . | 289 | 9.8 |
| 45 - 54. . . . . . | 185 | 6.3 |
| 55 - 64. . . . . . | 78 | 2.6 |
| 65 - over. . . . . . | 56 | 1.9 |

TABLE C.4.16

MONTHLY WAGES AND SALARY INCOME OF
EMPLOYED PERSONS 16 YEARS AND OLDER
(Cross-sectional)
(Unweighted Data)

| Income Level | N | % |
|---|---|---|
| Total. . . . . . . . . . . . . . . | 940 | 100.0 |
| Less than $200 . . . . . . . | 67 | 7.1 |
| 200 - 399. . . . . . . . | 158 | 16.8 |
| 400 - 599. . . . . . . . | 438 | 46.6 |
| 600 - 799. . . . . . . . | 170 | 18.1 |
| 800 - over . . . . . . . | 96 | 10.2 |
| Not ascertained. . . . . . | 11 | 1.2 |

## TABLE C.4.17

### DISTRIBUTION OF HOUSEHOLDS BY SIZE
(Cross-sectional)
(Unweighted Data)

| Household Size | N | % |
|---|---|---|
| Total. . . . . . . . | 645 | 100.0 |
| 1-person household . . . . . . . . | 127 | 19.7 |
| 2-person household . . . . . . . . | 77 | 11.9 |
| 3-person household . . . . . . . . | 72 | 11.2 |
| 4-person household . . . . . . . . | 78 | 12.1 |
| 5-person household . . . . . . . . | 63 | 9.8 |
| 6-person household . . . . . . . . | 61 | 9.5 |
| 7-person household . . . . . . . . | 51 | 7.9 |
| 8-person household . . . . . . . . | 40 | 6.2 |
| 9-person household . . . . . . . . | 32 | 5.0 |
| 10-person household . . . . . . . . | 20 | 3.1 |
| 11 or more persons in household . . | 24 | 3.7 |

TABLE C.4.18

DISTRIBUTION OF HOUSEHOLDS BY NUMBER OF
EMPLOYED PERSONS 16 YEARS AND OLDER
(Cross-sectional)
(Unweighted Data)

| Number of Employed Persons | Number of Households | % |
|---|---|---|
| Total. . . . . . . . . . . | 645 | 100.0 |
| With no employed person. . | 85 | 13.2 |
| With 1 person employed . . | 298 | 46.2 |
| With 2 persons employed. . | 185 | 28.7 |
| With 3 persons employed. . | 46 | 7.1 |
| With 4 persons employed. . | 23 | 3.6 |
| With 5 persons employed. . | 6 | .9 |
| With 6 or more employed. . | 2 | .3 |

## TABLE C.5.1

### LABOR FORCE PARTICIPATION OF PERSONS 16 YEARS AND OLDER BY SEX
#### (Weighted Percentages)

| Sex | Unweighted N | In Labor Force | Not in Labor Force |
|---|---|---|---|
| Total. . . . . | 1604 | 66.5 | 33.5 |
| Males. . . | 889 | 79.2 | 20.8 |
| Females. . . | 715 | 49.8 | 50.2 |

## TABLE C.5.2

### LABOR FORCE PARTICIPATION OF PERSONS 16 YEARS AND OLDER BY SEX AND RELATIONSHIP TO HEAD OF HOUSEHOLD
(Weighted Percentages)

| Relationship to Household Head | Males | | | | Females | | | |
|---|---|---|---|---|---|---|---|---|
| | Unweighted N | In Labor Force | | Not in Labor Force | Unweighted N | In Labor Force | | Not in Labor Force |
| | | Employed | Not Employed | | | Employed | Not Employed | |
| Total. . . . . . . | 889 | 75.3 | 3.9 | 20.8 | 715 | 46.4 | 3.4 | 50.2 |
| Head . . . . . . . | 533 | 83.0 | 4.9 | 12.0 | 74 | 71.2 | 5.8 | 23.0 |
| Spouse . . . . . . | 12 | 100.0 | - | - | 343 | 45.9 | 4.1 | 50.0 |
| Child or spouse of child . . . . | 162 | 53.3 | 1.6 | 45.1 | 145 | 47.1 | 3.7 | 49.2 |
| Grandchild/ nephew/niece . . | 12 | 78.8 | - | 21.2 | 13 | 36.9 | - | 63.2 |
| Parent or spouse . | 22 | 19.4 | - | 80.5 | 62 | 3.0 | - | 97.0 |
| Other relative . . | 88 | 63.2 | 5.0 | 31.8 | 77 | 56.7 | - | 43.3 |
| Unrelated/no answer . . . . . | 60 | 86.6 | 1.3 | 12.1 | 1 | - | - | 100.0 |

189

**TABLE** C.5.3

REASONS FOR NOT SEEKING EMPLOYMENT BY AGE AND SEX
(Weighted Percentages)

| Age and Sex | Unweighted N | Reasons Given | | | | | | |
|---|---|---|---|---|---|---|---|---|
| | | Attending School | Keeping House | Poor Health | Can Not Speak English | Other Means of Support | Dis- couraged | Other |
| Total. . . . . . | 545 | 48.2 | 29.8 | 21.3 | 9.1 | .5 | .4 | 3.1 |
| 16 - 24. . . . . | 226 | 84.9 | 12.9 | 3.1 | 1.4 | - | - | 1.2 |
| 25 - 34. . . . . | 98 | 32.4 | 59.9 | 7.4 | 3.3 | - | .8 | 4.1 |
| 35 - 44. . . . . | 58 | 35.7 | 58.3 | 2.8 | 7.6 | - | - | 7.3 |
| 45 and over. . . | 163 | 12.9 | 22.3 | 62.3 | 24.0 | 1.5 | 1.0 | 3.7 |
| Males. . . . . . | 184 | 77.1 | .8 | 16.0 | 7.0 | - | .4 | 6.3 |
| 16 - 24. . . . . | 100 | 98.4 | .8 | 2.0 | - | - | - | .8 |
| 25 - 34. . . . . | 28 | 75.1 | - | 11.1 | 8.5 | - | - | 13.7 |
| 35 - 44. . . . . | 14 | 77.8 | - | 5.5 | - | - | - | 16.7 |
| 45 and over. . . | 42 | 30.7 | 1.7 | 54.2 | 23.9 | - | 1.7 | 9.7 |
| Females. . . . . | 361 | 32.6 | 45.5 | 24.2 | 10.2 | .7 | .5 | 1.4 |
| 16 - 24. . . . . | 126 | 73.8 | 23.0 | 4.1 | 2.6 | - | - | 1.4 |
| 25 - 34. . . . . | 70 | 14.1 | 85.5 | 5.9 | 1.1 | - | 1.1 | - |
| 35 - 44. . . . . | 44 | 20.5 | 79.4 | 1.8 | 10.3 | - | - | 4.0 |
| 45 and over. . . | 121 | 6.0 | 30.2 | 65.5 | 24.0 | 2.1 | .7 | 1.4 |

**TABLE C.5.4**

EMPLOYMENT STATUS OF PERSONS 16 YEARS AND OLDER
BY PROFICIENCY IN ENGLISH
(Weighted Percentages)

| Proficiency in English | Unweighted N | Employed | Unemployed |
|---|---|---|---|
| Total. . . . . . . . | 1059 | 94.5 | 5.5 |
| **Understand English .** | | | |
| Not at all . . . . | 25 | 88.8 | 11.2 |
| Some . . . . . | 672 | 93.4 | 6.6 |
| Well . . . . . | 362 | 97.1 | 2.9 |
| **Speak English** | | | |
| Not at all . . . . | 27 | 90.1 | 9.9 |
| Some . . . . . | 681 | 93.5 | 6.5 |
| Well . . . . . | 351 | 97.0 | 3.0 |
| **Read English** | | | |
| Not at all . . . . | 38 | 92.3 | 7.7 |
| Some . . . . . | 689 | 93.4 | 6.6 |
| Well . . . . . | 332 | 97.3 | 2.7 |
| **Write English.** | | | |
| Not at all . . . . | 38 | 92.6 | 7.4 |
| Some . . . . . | 704 | 93.5 | 6.5 |
| Well . . . . . | 317 | 97.1 | 2.9 |

TABLE C.5.5

LABOR FORCE PARTICIPATION OF PERSONS 16 YEARS AND OLDER
BY PROFICIENCY IN ENGLISH
(Weighted Percentages)

| Proficiency in English | Unweighted N | In Labor Force | | Not in Labor Force |
|---|---|---|---|---|
| | | Employed | Unemployed | |
| Total . . . . . . . . | 1604 | 62.8 | 3.7 | 33.5 |
| **Understand English** | | | | |
| Not at all . . . . . | 131 | 17.7 | 2.2 | 80.0 |
| Some. . . . . . . . | 979 | 65.2 | 4.6 | 30.3 |
| Well. . . . . . . . | 494 | 70.8 | 2.1 | 27.1 |
| **Speak English** | | | | |
| Not at all. . . . . | 135 | 19.8 | 2.2 | 78.1 |
| Some. . . . . . . . | 987 | 65.4 | 4.5 | 30.0 |
| Well. . . . . . . . | 482 | 70.2 | 2.2 | 27.6 |
| **Read English** | | | | |
| Not at all. . . . . | 161 | 22.2 | 1.9 | 75.9 |
| Some. . . . . . . . | 988 | 65.9 | 4.7 | 29.4 |
| Well. . . . . . . . | 455 | 70.9 | 2.0 | 27.1 |
| **Write English** | | | | |
| Not at all. . . . . | 163 | 22.7 | 1.8 | 75.5 |
| Some. . . . . . . . | 1010 | 66.2 | 4.6 | 29.2 |
| Well. . . . . . . . | 431 | 70.9 | 2.1 | 27.1 |

192

**TABLE C.5.6**

EMPLOYMENT STATUS OF PERSONS 16 YEARS
AND OLDER BY AGE AND SEX
(Weighted Percentages)

| Age | Males | | | Females | | |
|---|---|---|---|---|---|---|
| | Unweighted N | Employed | Not Employed | Unweighted N | Employed | Not Employed |
| Total. . . . . | 705 | 95.1 | 4.9 | 354 | 93.2 | 6.8 |
| 16 - 24 . . | 217 | 95.2 | 4.8 | 113 | 93.1 | 6.9 |
| 25 - 34 . . | 238 | 95.7 | 4.3 | 129 | 95.6 | 4.4 |
| 35 - 44 . . | 140 | 97.5 | 2.5 | 81 | 96.7 | 3.3 |
| 45 - over. . | 110 | 90.6 | 9.4 | 31 | 73.3 | 26.7 |

## TABLE C.5.7

EMPLOYMENT STATUS OF PERSONS 16 YEARS AND OLDER
BY SEX AND RELATIONSHIP TO HEAD OF HOUSEHOLD
(Weighted Percentages)

| Relationship to Household Head | Males | | | Females | | |
|---|---|---|---|---|---|---|
| | Unweighted N | Employed | Not Employed | Unweighted N | Employed | Not Employed |
| Total. . . . . . . . | 705 | 95.1 | 4.9 | 354 | 93.2 | 6.8 |
| Head. . . . . . . . | 473 | 94.4 | 5.6 | 53 | 92.5 | 7.5 |
| Spouse. . . . . . . | 12 | 100.0 | - | 176 | 91.7 | 8.3 |
| Child or spouse of child. . . | 94 | 97.1 | 2.9 | 75 | 92.6 | 7.4 |
| Grandchild/ nephew/niece. . | 8 | 100.0 | - | 4 | 100.0 | - |
| Parent or spouse. . | 3 | 100.0 | - | 2 | 100.0 | - |
| Other relative. . | 60 | 92.7 | 7.3 | 44 | 100.0 | - |
| Unrelated/no answer. . . . . | 55 | 98.6 | 1.4 | - | - | - |

TABLE C.5.8

EMPLOYMENT STATUS OF HEADS OF HOUSEHOLD
BY SEX AND EDUCATIONAL ATTAINMENT
(Weighted Percentages)

| Education | Males | | | Females | | |
|---|---|---|---|---|---|---|
| | Unweighted N | Employed | Un-employed | Unweighted N | Employed | Un-employed |
| Total. . . . . . . | 473 | 94.4 | 5.6 | 53 | 92.5 | 7.5 |
| None . . . . . . | 72 | 89.8 | 10.2 | 11 | 100.0 | - |
| Primary Diploma. . | 37 | 91.0 | 9.0 | 4 | 100.0 | - |
| BEPSI/DEPSI/BE . . | 70 | 93.3 | 6.7 | 12 | 79.0 | 21.0 |
| BACC I . . . . . . | 32 | 92.2 | 7.8 | 7 | 100.0 | - |
| BACC II . . . . . | 173 | 97.7 | 2.3 | 14 | 94.8 | 5.2 |
| University . . . . | 81 | 94.9 | 5.1 | 5 | 100.0 | - |
| Other. . . . . . . | 8 | 100.0 | - | - | - | - |

PRIMARY DIPLOMA:

Elementary school diploma, awarded to those who pass an examination after
five years of schooling, from grade one through grade five.

BEPSI/DEPSI/BE:

Junior high school diploma, awarded to those who pass an examination after
their completion of the ninth grade.

BACC I and BACC II:

(Baccalaureate -- 1st part and 2nd part, respectively): awarded to those
who have successfully completed their 11th and 12th grades in secondary
school; generally considered as the main criteria in the selection of
candidates for mid-level positions in the government.  BACC II (Baccalaureate -- 2nd part) is a prerequisite for admission into college or
university.

195

**TABLE C.5.9**

EMPLOYMENT STATUS OF HEADS OF HOUSEHOLD
BY VIETNAM OCCUPATION
(Weighted Percentages)

| Vietnam Occupation | Unweighted N | Employed | Unemployed |
|---|---|---|---|
| Total . . . . . . . . . | 526 | 94.2 | 5.8 |
| White-Collar. . . . . . . | 335 | 96.2 | 3.8 |
| Professional. . . . . | 147 | 97.3 | 2.7 |
| Managers. . . . . . . | 76 | 94.1 | 5.9 |
| Clerical and Sales. . | 112 | 96.0 | 4.0 |
| Blue-Collar . . . . . . . | 191 | 92.0 | 8.0 |
| Craftsman . . . . . . | 73 | 93.0 | 7.0 |
| Operatives and Transport. . . . . . | 17 | 87.0 | 13.0 |
| Laborers. . . . . . . | 74 | 92.4 | 7.6 |
| Other Blue-Collar . . | 27 | 86.2 | 13.8 |

**TABLE C.5.10**

HOURS WORKED PER WEEK BY AGE AND SEX
(Weighted Percentages)

| Age and Sex | Unweighted N | Hours Worked Per Week | | | |
|---|---|---|---|---|---|
| | | Less than 15 | 15 – 29 | 30 – 39 | 40 or more |
| Total . . . . . | 998 | 1.3 | 10.3 | 4.3 | 84.1 |
| 16 – 24 . . . | 313 | 3.7 | 20.8 | 4.4 | 71.0 |
| 25 – 34 . . . | 351 | .2 | 5.6 | 4.4 | 89.8 |
| 35 – 44 . . . | 214 | – | 6.8 | 4.7 | 88.6 |
| 45 and over . | 120 | .7 | 3.3 | 2.5 | 93.5 |
| Males . . . . . | 669 | 1.4 | 8.4 | 3.4 | 86.8 |
| 16 – 24 . . . | 207 | 4.1 | 21.3 | 4.1 | 70.5 |
| 25 – 34 . . . | 229 | – | 3.7 | 3.8 | 92.4 |
| 35 – 44 . . . | 136 | – | 2.1 | 2.5 | 95.4 |
| 45 and over . | 97 | .8 | 1.6 | 1.6 | 96.0 |
| Females . . . . | 329 | 1.2 | 14.2 | 6.2 | 78.3 |
| 16 – 24 . . . | 106 | 2.9 | 19.9 | 5.1 | 72.0 |
| 25 – 34 . . . | 122 | .7 | 9.2 | 5.6 | 84.5 |
| 35 – 44 . . . | 78 | – | 15.5 | 8.7 | 75.9 |
| 45 and over . | 23 | – | 11.1 | 6.9 | 82.1 |

**TABLE C.5.11**

HOURS WORKED PER WEEK BY WEEKLY WAGES AND SALARY INCOME
(Weighted Percentages)

| Hours Per Week | Weighted N | Weekly Wages and Salary Income | | | | | | |
|---|---|---|---|---|---|---|---|---|
| | | Less than $50 | $50-99 | $100-124 | $125-149 | $150-174 | $175-199 | $200-more |
| Total . . . . . . | 998 | 6.2 | 16.2 | 25.6 | 18.0 | 13.7 | 6.0 | 14.3 |
| Less than 15 . . | 17 | 93.8 | 6.2 | - | - | - | - | - |
| 15 - 29. . . . | 103 | 31.6 | 59.2 | 8.4 | .8 | - | - | - |
| 30 - 39. . . . . | 44 | - | 50.9 | 20.4 | 12.7 | 12.1 | 3.8 | - |
| 40 or more . . . | 834 | 2.0 | 9.3 | 28.4 | 20.6 | 15.6 | 6.9 | 17.0 |

198

**TABLE C.5.12**

PROFICIENCY IN ENGLISH BY WEEKLY WAGES AND SALARY INCOME

(Weighted Percentages)

| Proficiency in English | Unweighted N | Weekly Wages and Salary Income | | | | | | |
|---|---|---|---|---|---|---|---|---|
| | | Less than $50 | $50-99 | $100-124 | $125-149 | $150-174 | $175-199 | $200-more |
| Total . . . . . . . | 998 | 6.2 | 16.2 | 25.6 | 18.0 | 13.7 | 6.0 | 14.3 |
| Understand English | | | | | | | | |
| Not at all . . . . | 21 | 3.1 | 35.7 | 30.8 | 19.0 | 6.9 | - | 3.6 |
| Some . . . . . | 628 | 5.3 | 15.3 | 30.3 | 19.2 | 14.7 | 4.8 | 10.4 |
| Well . . . . . | 349 | 8.1 | 16.6 | 16.2 | 15.5 | 12.2 | 8.7 | 22.6 |
| Speak English | | | | | | | | |
| Not at all . . . . | 23 | 2.7 | 44.0 | 26.8 | 17.3 | 6.0 | - | 3.2 |
| Some . . . . . | 637 | 5.2 | 15.1 | 29.7 | 19.2 | 15.0 | 4.9 | 10.9 |
| Well . . . . . | 338 | 8.4 | 16.1 | 17.3 | 15.5 | 11.7 | 8.8 | 22.2 |
| Read English . . . . | | | | | | | | |
| Not at all . . . . | 34 | 2.1 | 28.1 | 34.3 | 24.2 | 6.8 | - | 4.5 |
| Some . . . . . | 643 | 5.2 | 15.4 | 29.6 | 18.4 | 15.0 | 5.4 | 11.1 |
| Well . . . . . | 321 | 8.8 | 16.5 | 16.2 | 16.2 | 11.7 | 8.1 | 22.4 |
| Write English | | | | | | | | |
| Not at all . . . . | 34 | 2.0 | 33.7 | 32.6 | 23.0 | 6.5 | - | 2.3 |
| Some . . . . . | 658 | 5.1 | 15.4 | 29.1 | 18.1 | 15.3 | 5.8 | 11.2 |
| Well . . . . . | 306 | 9.4 | 15.7 | 18.1 | 15.3 | 11.0 | 7.3 | 23.2 |

TABLE C.5.13

MONTHLY HOUSEHOLD INCOME FROM ALL SOURCES
BY COMPONENTS OF INCOME

(Percent of Households Deriving Income From Each Source)
(Weighted Percentages)

| Household Income (All Sources) | Unweighted N | Percent of Households Deriving Income From Each Source | | | |
|---|---|---|---|---|---|
| | | Wage and Salary Income | Refugee Financial Assistance* | SSI* | Other Financial Contributions* |
| Total . . . . . . . . | 607 | 89.0 | 20.9 | 7.4 | 6.8 |
| Under $200. . . . | 17 | 41.1 | 55.2 | - | 3.7 |
| $200 to $399. . . | 39 | 54.4 | 32.4 | 9.0 | 12.4 |
| $400 to $599. . . | 111 | 90.0 | 21.3 | 3.5 | 5.6 |
| $600 to $799. . . | 86 | 95.9 | 24.7 | 7.5 | 4.9 |
| $800 or more. . . | 336 | 100.0 | 17.1 | 9.5 | 7.6 |
| Not Ascertained . | 18 | - | - | - | - |

*Assistance was reported as being received at the time of the interview.

200

## TABLE C.5.14

### MONTHLY HOUSEHOLD INCOME FROM ALL SOURCES
(Weighted Percentages)

| Income Level | Households with Income | |
| --- | --- | --- |
| | Unweighted N | % |
| Total. . . . . . | 607 | 100.0 |
| Under $200 . . . | 17 | 3.2 |
| $200 - 399 . . . | 39 | 7.8 |
| $400 - 599 . . . | 111 | 20.6 |
| $600 - 799 . . . | 86 | 14.0 |
| $800 - over. . . | 336 | 51.4 |
| Not Ascertained. . | 18 | 3.1 |

**TABLE C.5.15**

FEDERAL ASSISTANCE RECEIVED BY REFUGEE HOUSEHOLDS
(Weighted Percentages)

| Type of Federal Assistance* | Households Receiving | |
|---|---|---|
| | Unweighted N | Weighted % |
| Total. . . . . . . . . . | 607 | 100.0 |
| Number of households receiving one or more types of Federal assistance . | 201 | 32.0 |
| Food Stamps. . . . . . . | 138 | 22.8 |
| Refugee Financial Assistance . . . . . | 131 | 20.9 |
| SSI. . . . . . . . | 50 | 7.4 |

*Assistance was reported as being received at the time of the interview. In addition, a household may at the same time receive more than one type of federal assistance.

**TABLE C.5.16**

DISTRIBUTION OF JOB-HUNTING METHODS OF UNEMPLOYED
REFUGEES BY AGE

(Weighted Percentages)

| Age | Unweighted N | Job-Hunting Methods* | | | | | |
|---|---|---|---|---|---|---|---|
| | | Contact Employer | Contact Employment Agencies | Through Friend/ Relative | Through Sponsor | Answer Ads | Place Ads |
| Total. . . | 61 | 66.5 | 61.4 | 26.9 | 2.8 | 23.9 | 1.3 |
| 16-24. . | 17 | 80.7 | 72.7 | 15.8 | – | 35.2 | – |
| 25-34. . | 16 | 59.9 | 60.0 | 25.8 | 9.7 | 30.7 | – |
| 35-44. . | 7 | 57.8 | 70.9 | 28.7 | – | 14.3 | – |
| 45-over. | 21 | 60.7 | 47.8 | 39.0 | – | 8.6 | 4.3 |

*Each person may use more than one of these methods in job-hunting.

**TABLE C.5.17**

DISTRIBUTION OF HOUSEHOLDS BY REGION
(Weighted Percentages)

| Region | Unweighted N | % |
|---|---|---|
| Total. . . . . . . . . . . . | 607 | 100.0 |
| North-eastern Region . . . | 88 | 14.9 |
| Western Region . . . . | 202 | 32.8 |
| North-central Region . . . | 137 | 21.5 |
| Southern Region. . . . . | 180 | 30.8 |

# TABLE C.5.18

## DISTRIBUTION OF REFUGEES BY AGE
### (Weighted Percentages)

| Age | Unweighted N | % |
|---|---|---|
| Total. . . . . . . . . . . . . . . | 2817 | 100.0 |
| 0 - 4. . . | 379 | 13.6 |
| 5 - 14. . . | 762 | 26.9 |
| 15 - 24. . . | 628 | 22.0 |
| 25 - 34. . . | 465 | 17.8 |
| 35 - 44. . . | 279 | 9.4 |
| 45 - 54. . . | 173 | 5.9 |
| 55 - 64. . . | 77 | 2.5 |
| 65 - over. . . | 54 | 1.9 |

205

TABLE C.5.19

DISTRIBUTION OF REFUGEES BY AGE AND SEX
(Weighted Percentages)

| Age and Sex | Unweighted N | % |
|---|---|---|
| Total . . . . . . . . | 2817 | 100.0 |
| Males . . . . . . . | 1526 | 54.8 |
| 0 - 4 . . . . . | 196 | 12.3 |
| 5 - 14 . . . . . | 405 | 26.5 |
| 15 - 24 . . . . . | 353 | 22.7 |
| 25 - 34 . . . . . | 266 | 19.1 |
| 35 - 44 . . . . . | 154 | 9.7 |
| 45 - 54 . . . . . | 95 | 6.0 |
| 55 - 64 . . . . . | 39 | 2.3 |
| 65 - over . . . . | 18 | 1.4 |
| Females . . . . . . | 1291 | 45.2 |
| 0 - 4 . . . . . | 183 | 15.2 |
| 5 - 14 . . . . . | 357 | 27.3 |
| 15 - 24 . . . . . | 275 | 21.1 |
| 25 - 34 . . . . . | 199 | 16.2 |
| 35 - 44 . . . . . | 125 | 9.0 |
| 45 - 54 . . . . . | 78 | 5.8 |
| 55 - 64 . . . . . | 38 | 2.8 |
| 65 - over . . . . | 36 | 2.6 |

**TABLE C.5.20**

DISTRIBUTION OF HEADS OF HOUSEHOLD
BY SEX AND EDUCATIONAL ATTAINMENT
(Weighted Percentages)

| Education | Unweighted N | Male | | Female | |
|---|---|---|---|---|---|
| | | N | % | N | % |
| Total. . . . . . . . | 607 | 533 | 87.1 | 74 | 12.9 |
| None . . . . . . . | 107 | 85 | 83.3 | 22 | 16.7 |
| Primary Diploma. . . | 49 | 42 | 86.6 | 7 | 13.4 |
| BEPSI/DEPSI/BE . . . | 94 | 80 | 80.6 | 14 | 19.4 |
| BACC. I. . . . . . . | 45 | 38 | 80.6 | 7 | 19.4 |
| BACC. II . . . . . . | 208 | 190 | 90.9 | 18 | 9.1 |
| University . . . . . | 96 | 90 | 93.4 | 6 | 6.6 |
| Other. . . . . . . . | 8 | 8 | 100.0 | - | - |

PRIMARY DIPLOMA:

Elementary school diploma, awarded to those who pass an examination after
five years of schooling, from grade one through grade five.

BEPSI/DEPSI/BE:

Junior high school diploma, awarded to those who pass an examination after
their completion of the ninth grade.

BACC I and BACC II:

(Baccalaureate--1st part and 2nd part, respectively): awarded to those
who have successfully completed their 11th and 12th grades in secondary
school; generally considered as the main criteria in the selection of
candidates for mid-level positions in the government. BACC II (Baccalau-
reate--2nd part) is a prerequiste for admission into college or university.

207

## TABLE C.5.21

DISTRIBUTION OF HOUSEHOLDS BY NUMBER OF
EMPLOYED PERSONS 16 YEARS AND OLDER
(Weighted Percentages)

| Number of Employed Persons | Number of Households | % |
|---|---|---|
| Total. . . . . . . . . . . . | 607 | 100.0 |
| With no employed person. . . | 62 | 11.0 |
| With 1 person employed . . . | 246 | 43.3 |
| With 2 persons employed. . . | 212 | 33.1 |
| With 3 persons employed. . . | 47 | 7.3 |
| With 4 persons employed. . . | 22 | 3.0 |
| With 5 persons employed. . . | 14 | 1.9 |
| With 6 or more employed. . . | 4 | .5 |

208

# Bibliography

My search for materials on Vietnamese in America at the Library of Congress made me aware of the paucity of literature on this subject. Thus, this bibliography includes not only the materials cited in the text of this volume, but also represents an initial attempt to develop a research bibliography. The reader will note that some references to research on Vietnamese in America are included even though in many cases they are only tangentially related to the central theme of this volume. While this clearly is not a complete bibliography on the Vietnamese in America, it does represent one step in filling the void.

BAIN, CHESTER A.
    1967    *Vietnam: The Roots of Conflict.* Englewood Cliffs, N.J.: Prentice-Hall.

BONACICH, EDNA
    1973    "A Theory of Middleman Minorities." *American Sociological Review* 38 (October):583-94.

BROWN, L. DEAN
    1975    "Relief and Resettlement of Vietnamese and Cambodian Refugees." *Department of State Bulletin* 72 (June 2):741-5.

BRYCE-LAPORTE, ROY S. AND STEPHEN COUCH (EDS.)
1976    *Exploratory Field Work on Latino Migrants and Indochinese Refugees.* Washington, D.C.: Research Institute on Immigration and Ethnic Studies, Research Notes No. 1, Smithsonian Institution.

BUTTINGER, JOSEPH
1958    *The Smaller Dragon: A Political History of Vietnam.* New York: Praeger.

1968    *Vietnam: A Political History.* New York: Praeger.

1972    *A Dragon Defiant: A Short History of Vietnam.* New York: Praeger.

CALIFORNIA STATE UNIVERSITY
1968    *Vietnam: Bibliography.* Sacramento, California: University Library.

CENTER FOR APPLIED LINGUISTICS
n.d.    *Education in Vietnam: Fundamental Principles and Curricula.* Arlington, Virginia: Center for Applied Linguistics.

n.d.    *On Assimilating Vietnamese and Cambodian Students into United States Schools.* Arlington, Virginia: Center for Applied Linguistics.

n.d.    *On Keeping Lines of Communication with Indochinese Children Open.* Arlington, Virginia: Center for Applied Linguistics.

n.d.    *A Personnel Resources Directory for the Education of Vietnamese Refugees.* Arlington, Virginia: Center for Applied Linguistics.

n.d.    *A Selected Annotated Bibliography for Teaching English to Speakers of Vietnamese.* Arlington, Virginia: Center for Applied Linguistics.

n.d.    *Vietnamese History, Literature and Folklore.* Arlington, Virginia: Center for Applied Linguistics.

CHAPMAN, WILLIAM
1978a   "Malaysia Reels Under Refugee Tide." *The Washington Post* (December 11):A-1 and A-20.

1978b   "Refugee Waves Turn Malaysians Hostile." *The Washington Post* (December 12):A-15.

COOKE, DAVID C.
1968    *Vietnam: The Country, The People.* New York: Grosset and Dunlop.

CRAWFORD, ANN
    1966    *Customs and Culture of Vietnam.* Rutland, Vermont: Charles E. Tuttle.

DEVILLERS, PHILIPPE
    1953    "Vietnamese Nationalism and French Politics." In Wm. L. Holland (ed.), *Asian Nationalism and the West.* New York: MacMillan.

DILLMAN, DON A.
    1978    *Mail and Telephone Surveys: The Total Design Method.* New York: Wiley.

DOAN, HAN T.
    1977    "Factors that Foster or Impede the Process of Acculturation of Vietnamese Refugees." Paper presented at the annual meeting of the American Sociological Association, Chicago, Illinois.

DULING, GRETCHEN A.
    1977    *Adopting Joe: A Black Vietnamese Child.* Rutland, Vt.: Charles E. Tuttle.

DUONG THANH BINH
    n.d.    *A Handbook for Teachers of Vietnamese Students.* Arlington, Virginia: Center for Applied Linguistics.

DUONG THIEU TONG
    1968    "A Proposal for the Comprehensive Secondary School Curriculum in Vietnam." Ph.D. Dissertation, Teachers College, Columbia Uuiversity.

FALK, RICHARD A. (ED.)
    1968    *The Vietnam War and International Law.* Princeton, New Jersey: Princeton University Press.

FALL, BERNARD B.
    1967    *The Two Vietnams, A Political and Military Analysis.* New York: Praeger.

GOLDLUST, JOHN AND ANTHONY H. RICHMOND
    1974    "A Multivariate Model of Immigrant Adaptation." *International Migration Review* 8 (2) (Summer):193-225.

GORDON, MILTON M.
    1964    *Assimilation in American Life.* New York: Oxford University Press.

    1975    "Toward a General Theory of Racial and Ethnic Group Relations." Pp. 84-110 in *Ethnicity,* N. Glazer and D. P. Moynihan (Eds.). Cambridge: Harvard University Press.

GROUSSET, RENE
    1953    *The Rise and Splendor of the Chinese Empire.* Berkeley,
            California: University of California Press.

HALL, DANIEL G. E.
    1955    *A History of South-East Asia.* New York: St. Martins
            Press.

    1964    *A History of South-East Asia.* (2nd Edition) New York:
            St. Martins Press.

HAMMER, ELLEN
    1954    *The Struggle for Indochina.* (First Edition) Stanford,
            California: Stanford University Press.

    1966a   *The Struggle for Indochina, 1940-1955.* Stanford, Cali-
            fornia: Stanford University Press.

    1966b   *Vietnam Yesterday and Today.* New York: Holt, Rinehart
            and Winston.

HEISS, JEROLD
    1969    "Factors Related to Immigrant Assimilation: Premigration
            Traits." *Social Forces* 47 (June):422-428.

HENDERSON, LARRY
    1967    *Vietnam and Countries of the Mekong.* (Revised Edition)
            New York: Thomas Nelson.

HICKEY, GERALD G.
    1960    *The Study of a Vietnamese Rural Community.* East
            Lansing, Michigan: Department of Sociology, Michigan
            State University Press.

    1964    *Village in Vietnam.* New Haven, Connecticut: Yale Uni-
            versity Press.

HIRAYAMA, HISACHI
    1977    "A Study of Vietnamese Refugees in Western Tennessee
            and Arkansas: Their Socioeconomic Status, Problems, and
            Service Needs." Paper presented at the Annual Meeting of
            Council on Social Work Education.

HOHL, DONALD G.
    1978    "The Indochinese Refugee: The Evolution of United States
            Policy." *International Migration Review* 12 (Spring):128-
            132.

HUARD, PIERRE AND MAURICE DURAND
    1954    *Connaissance du Viet-nam.* Paris and Hanoi: *Imprimerie
            National, l'Ecole Francaise d'extrême Orient.*

Ichihashi, Y.
  1932    *Japanese in the United States.* Stanford, California: Stanford University Press.

Isaacs, Harold
  1947    *No Peace in Asia.* New York: MacMillan.

Justus, Joyce Bennett
  1976    "Processing Indochinese Refugees." Pp. 76-100 in Roy S. Bryce-Laporte and Stephen R. Couch (eds.), *Exploratory Fieldwork on Latino Migrants and Indochinese Refugees.* Washington, D.C.: RIIES Research Notes No. 1, Smithsonian Institution.

Kelly, Gail Paradise
  1977    *From Vietnam to America: A Chronicle of the Vietnamese Immigration to the United States.* Boulder, Colorado: Westview Press.

  1978    "Adult Education for Vietnamese Refugees: Commentary on Pluralism in America." *Journal of Ethnic Studies* 5 (Winter):55-64.

Kitano, Harry H. L.
  1976    *Japanese Americans: The Evolution of a Subculture.* Englewood Cliffs, New Jersey: Prentice-Hall.

Kneeland, Douglas E.
  1975    "Wide Hostility Found to Vietnamese Influx." *The New York Times* (May 2):A-1, Col. 1.

  1977    "Skilled Jobs Elude a Well-Trained Refugee." *The New York Times* (February 28):16, Col. 3.

Kunz, E. F.
  1973    "The Refugees in Flight: Kinetic Models and Forms of Displacement." *International Migration Review* 7:125-46.

Lee, Everett S.
  1969    "A Theory of Migration." Pp. 286-7 in J. A. Jackson (ed.), *Migration.* Cambridge: Cambridge University Press.

Levine, Gene N. and Darrel Montero
  1973    "Socioeconomic Mobility among Three Generations of Japanese Americans." *Journal of Social Issues* 29(2): 33-48.

Light, Ivan H.
  1972    *Ethnic Enterprise in America: Business and Welfare Among Chinese, Japanese, and Blacks.* Berkeley, Los Angeles, London: University of California Press.

213

LIU, WILLIAM T. AND ALICE K. MURATTA
    1977a    "The Vietnamese in America: Refugees or Immigrants?" *Bridge: An Asian American Perspective* 5 (3) (Fall):31-39.

    1977b    "The Vietnamese in America, Part II: Perilous Flights, Uncertain Future." *Bridge: An Asian American Perspective* 5 (4) (Winter):42-50.

    1978a    "The Vietnamese in America, Part III: Life in the Refugee Camps." *Bridge: An Asian American Perspective* 6 (1) (Spring):36-46.

    1978b    "The Vietnamese in America, Part IV: Mental Health of Vietnamese Refugees." *Bridge: An Asian American Perspective* 6 (2) (Summer):44-49.

LYMAN, STANFORD M.
    1974    *Chinese Americans.* New York: Random House.

MASSON, ANDRE
    1960    *Histoire du Vietnam.* Paris: Presses Universitaires de France.

MIYAMOTO, S. FRANK
    1939    "Social Solidarity among the Japanese in Seattle." *University of Washington Publications in the Social Sciences* 11 (December):57-130.

MONTERO, DARREL
    1976    "Response Effects in the Use of the Mail Questionnaire and the Face-to-Face Interview among a National Sample of Japanese Americans." Paper presented at the annual meeting of the American Sociological Association, New York.

    1978a    "The Japanese American Community: A Study of Changing Patterns of Ethnic Affiliation over Three Generations." Revised Ph.D. Dissertation. University of California, Los Angeles.

    1978b    "Patterns of Racial Intermarriage among Three Generations of Japanese Americans." Unpublished Manuscript. University of Maryland, College Park.

    1979    "The Vietnamese Refugees in America: Patterns of Socioeconomic Adaptation and Assimilation." Unpublished manuscript, University of Maryland, College Park.

MONTERO, DARREL AND GENE N. LEVINE (EDS.)
    1977    "Research among Racial and Cultural Minorities: Problems, Prospects and Pitfalls." *Journal of Social Issues* 33 (4):1-222.

MURFIN, GARY DEAN
  1975    *War, Life and Stress: The Forced Relocation of the Viet-namese People.* Honolulu, Hawaii: University of Hawaii Press.

NUNN, RAYMOND G.
  1971    *Asia: A Selected and Annotated Guide to Reference Works.* Cambridge, Massachusetts: M.I.T. Press.

OPPORTUNITY SYSTEMS, INC.
  1975    *First Wave Report, Vietnam Resettlement Operational Feedback.* Washington, D.C.: Opportunity Systems, Inc., Contract No. HEW-100-76-0042. October 2.

  1976a   *Second Wave Report, Vietnam Resettlement Operational Feedback.* Washington, D.C.: Opportunity Systems, Inc., January.

  1976b   *Third Wave Report, Vietnam Resettlement Operational Feedback.* Washington, D.C.: Opportunity Systems, Inc., September.

  1977a   *Fourth Wave Report, Vietnam Resettlement Operational Feedback.* Washington, D.C.: Opportunity Systems, Inc., September.

  1977b   *Fifth Wave Report, Vietnam Resettlement Operational Feedback.* Washington, D.C.: Opportunity Systems, Inc., October.

PETERSEN, WILLIAM
  1958    "A General Typology of Migration." *American Sociological Review* 23 (June):256-66.

  1978    "International Migration." Pp. 533-75 in Ralph H. Turner, James Coleman, and Renée C. Fox (Eds.), *Annual Review of Sociology* 4. Palo Alto, California: Annual Reviews, Inc.

POOLE, PETER A.
  1973    *The United States and Indochina, From FDR to Nixon.* Hinsdale, Illinois: Dryden Press.

QUE, L. T., A. T. RANBO AND G. D. MURFIN
  1976    "Why They Fled: Refugee Movement during the Spring 1975 Communist Offensive in South Vietnam." *Asian Studies* (XVI) (9) (September):855-863.

RAGAS, WADE R. AND VINCENT MARUGGI
  1978    "Vietnamese Refugee Living Conditions in the New Orleans Metro Area." Working Paper No. 111. New Orleans, Louisiana: Division of Business and Economic Review, University of New Orleans.

215

RAHE, RICHARD H., JOHN G. LOONEY, HAROLD W. WARD, TRAN MINH
TUNG, AND WILLIAM T. LIU
1978 "Psychiatric Consultation in a Vietnamese Refugee Camp."
*American Journal of Psychiatry* 135(2) (February):185-90.

RICHMOND, ANTHONY H. AND RAVI P. VERMA
1978 "The Economic Adaptation of Immigrants: A New Theoretical Perspective." *International Migration Review* 12(1)
(Spring):3-38.

ROBINSON, CHRISTINE EMILE
1976 "Survey of Social Conditions of Vietnamese Refugee Families in San Francisco." Center for Southeast Asian Refugee Resettlement.

1977 "The Uses of Order and Disorder in Play: An Analysis
of Vietnamese Refugee Children's Play." *Association for
the Anthropological Study of Play Newsletter* 4(2) (Fall):
9-14.

ROSE, ARNOLD M. AND LEON WARSHAY
1957 "The Adjustment of Migrants to Cities." *Social Forces*
36 (October):72-76.

RUEBENSAAL, ANN PETERS
1978 "The Adjustment of Vietnamese Refugees to American
Culture." Unpublished manuscript, American University.

SLOTE, WALTER H.
1972 "Psychodynamic Structures in Vietnamese Personality." In
William Lebra (Ed.), *Transcultural Research in Mental
Health*. Honolulu: University of Hawaii Press.

1977 "Adaptation of Recent Vietnamese Immigrants to the
American Experience: A Psychocultural Approach." Pa-
per presented at the annual meeting of the Association for
Asian Studies, New York, March 27.

SMITH, RALPH BERNARD
1971 *Vietnam and the West*. Ithaca, New York: Cornell University Press.

SUDMAN, SEYMOUR AND NORMAN M. BRADBURN
1974 *Response Effects in Surveys*. Chicago: Aldine.

TRAN TUONG NHU
1976 "Vietnamese Refugees: The Trauma of Exile." *Civil
Rights Digest* 9(1) (Fall):59-62.

U.S., CONGRESS, SENATE
1955 *Vietnam, Cambodia and Laos: Report by Senator Mike
Mansfield*. Committee on Foreign Relations. Washington,
D.C.: U.S. Government Printing Office, October 6.

216

1975 *Hearings Held before the Senate Subcommittee to Investigate Problems Connected with Refugees and Escapees.* 94th Congress, 1st Session. Washington, D.C.: U.S. Government Printing Office, July.

1978 *Humanitarian Problems of Southeast Asia, 1977-1978.* Report by the Committee on the Judiciary. Washington, D.C.: U.S. Government Printing Office, March.

U.S. DEPARTMENT OF HEALTH, EDUCATION, AND WELFARE

1976a *HEW Refugee Task Force. Report to the Congress* Washington, D.C.: U.S. DHEW, March 15.

1976b *HEW Refugee Task Force. Report to the Congress.* Washington, D.C.: U.S. DHEW, June 15.

1976c *HEW Refugee Task Force. Report to the Congress.* Washington, D.C.: U.S. DHEW, September 20.

1976d *HEW Refugee Task Force. Report to the Congress.* Washington, D.C.: U.S. DHEW, December 20.

1977a *HEW Refugee Task Force. Report to the Congress.* Washington, D.C.: U.S. DHEW, March 21.

1977b *HEW Refugee Task Force. Report to the Congress.* Washington, D.C.: U.S. DHEW, June 20.

1977c *HEW Refugee Task Force. Report to the Congress.* Washington, D.C.: U.S. DHEW, September 21.

1977d *HEW Refugee Task Force. Report to the Congress.* Washington, D.C.: U.S. DHEW, December 31.

U.S. DEPARTMENT OF STATE

1975a *Interagency Task Force on Indochina Refugees. Report to the Congress.* Washington, D.C.: U.S. Department of State, June 15.

1975b *Interagency Task Force on Indochina Refugees. Report to the Congress.* Washington, D.C.: U.S. Department of State, September 15.

1975c *Interagency Task Force on Indochina Refugees. Report to the Congress.* Washington, D.C.: U.S. Department of State, December 15.

WEINTRAUB, RICHARD M.

1978 "Asia's Refugees: A New Wave of Human Migration." *The Washington Post* (December 12):A-1, A-14.

WEISS, MELFORD S.

1974 *Valley City: A Chinese Community In America.* Cambridge, Massachusetts: Schenkman.

WISEMAN, STANLEY F.
    1976    "Field Study Problems in a Refugee Camp: Community and Bureaucracy Compounded and Confounded." Pp.101-129 in Roy S. Bryce-Laporte and Stephen R. Couch (Eds.), *Exploratory Fieldwork on Latino Migrants and Indochinese Refugees.* RIIES Research Notes No. 1. Washington, D.C.: Smithsonian Institution.

YEE, BARBARA AND PETER W. VAN ARSDALE
    1978    "Breakdowns in Traditional Culture and the Effects of Learned Helplessness among Vietnamese Elderly." Paper presented at annual meetings of the Society for Applied Anthropology, Merida, Yucatan, Mexico, April 2-9.